Billy Graham
Evangelistic Association

Dear Friend,

I am pleased to send you this copy of *The Best Is Yet to Come* by my good friend Greg Laurie.

Whether you need encouragement in the trials you face today or certainty for an uncertain future, this book is a powerful reminder that when you know Jesus Christ personally, you can have peace and joy, no matter your circumstances. I pray that you will find security in Christ as you read this book and be able to truly say, "The best is yet to come."

For nearly 60 years, the Billy Graham Evangelistic Association has worked to take the Good News of Jesus Christ throughout the world by every effective means available, and I'm excited about what God will do in the years ahead. If you would like to know more about our ministry, please contact us:

In the U.S.:

Billy Graham Evangelistic Association
1 Billy Graham Parkway
Charlotte, North Carolina 28201-0001
www.billygraham.org
Toll-free: 1-877-2GRAHAM
(1-877-247-2426)

In Canada:

Billy Graham Evangelistic Association of Canada
20 Hopewell Way NE
Calgary, Alberta T3J 5H5
www.billygraham.ca
Toll-free: 1-888-393-0003

We would appreciate knowing how this book or our ministry has touched your life. May God bless you.

Sincerely,

Franklin Graham
President

THE BEST IS YET TO COME

~~~~~~~

GREG LAURIE

This **Billy Graham Library Selection** is published
by the Billy Graham Evangelistic Association
with permission from Multnomah Publishers.

Multnomah® Publishers *Sisters, Oregon*

Published by the Billy Graham Evangelistic Association
with permission from Multnomah Publishers.

A Billy Graham Library Selection designates materials that are
appropriate for a well-rounded collection of quality Christian literature,
including both classic and contemporary reading and reference materials.

THE BEST IS YET TO COME
published by Multnomah Publishers, Inc.

Cover design by Studiogearbox.com
Cover image Johner/Photonica

Unless otherwise indicated, Scripture quotations are from:

The Holy Bible, New King James Version © 1984 by Thomas Nelson, Inc.
Other Scripture quotations are from:
Holy Bible, New Living Translation (NLT) © 1996. Used by permission of
Tyndale House Publishers, Inc. All rights reserved.
The Holy Bible, New International Version (NIV) © 1973, 1984 by International Bible Society,
used by permission of Zondervan Publishing House
The New Testament in Modern English, Revised Edition (Phillips)
© 1958, 1960, 1972 by J. B. Phillips
The Holy Bible, English Standard Version (ESV)
© 2001 by Crossway Bibles, a division of Good News Publishers.
Used by permission. All rights reserved.

Multnomah is a trademark of Multnomah Publishers, Inc.,
and is registered in the U.S. Patent and Trademark Office.
The colophon is a trademark of Multnomah Publishers, Inc.

Printed in the United States of America

For information:
MULTNOMAH PUBLISHERS, INC. • 601 NORTH LARCH STREET • SISTERS, OR 97759

ISBN 1-59328-092-0
Previous: ISBN 1-59052-332-6

CONTENTS

THE BEST IS YET TO COME

IT'S FUNNY HOW OUR VIEWS OF AGING CHANGE AS we grow older.

Take, for instance, this illustration I heard recently:

When you were a kid and someone asked, "So how old are you?" you would say, "I'm five and a half." And you'd try to hold up five and a half fingers. You'll probably never hear an adult say, "I'm forty-six and a half." For some reason, grown-ups just don't get as excited as kids about those half- or three-quarter-year milestones.

Then when you got a little bit older and started

moving into those teen years, you would say, "I'm *going to be* sixteen." (You might only be twelve at the time.) Then adulthood finally arrives, and you "*become* twenty-one." Very official sounding. You become twenty-one, but then you blink your eyes and you find that you're *turning* thirty. What's happened here? You become twenty-one, you turn thirty, and then you're *pushing* forty! You become twenty-one, turn thirty, are pushing forty, and—before you know it—you *reach* fifty. Then you *make it* to sixty. Then you build up so much speed that you *hit* seventy.

After that, it's a day-to-day thing.

You go from your seventies to your eighties, and then it's, "I hit Wednesday." Then as you get even older, "I hit lunch today." Then you hit the century mark and you clear it. Someone says, "How old are you?" And you say, "I'm 101 and a half!"

There's no question that we live in a youth-obsessed culture. Everything seems to center around young people and what they have to say and what they think about this or that. And sometimes those of us who are getting a bit on in years feel as though we're not as relevant as we could be.

It had to happen.

We baby boomers are finally coming of age. The generation that said, "Don't trust anyone over thirty," is now stepping, incredulous and amazed, into its golden years. How could it be? Where in the world did the years go?

We try to relive our youth.

We keep telling ourselves we're still young (at heart).

We turn on the radio, maybe to our favorite oldies station, and we hear the old Leo Sayer number "You Make Me Feel like Dancing." Only we feel like it should be updated to "You Make Me Feel like Napping."

When you think about it, there are a number of those old sixties and seventies hits that could be revised a little for the benefit of aging baby boomers. For instance, Abba's "Dancing Queen" from my generation could become "Denture Queen."

Remember Herman's Hermits from the British Invasion of the sixties? Their classic "Mrs. Brown, You've Got a Lovely Daughter" could now be "Mrs. Brown, You've Got a Lovely Walker."

The Bee Gees's "How Can You Mend a Broken

Heart?" could morph into "How Can You Mend a Broken Hip?"

Remember Crystal Gayle's song "Don't It Make My Brown Eyes Blue"? Maybe we could retitle it "Don't It Make My Brown Hair Blue."

The old Jerry Lee Lewis classic "A Whole Lot of Shakin' Goin' On" could become "A Whole Lot of Achin' Goin' On."

And we can't forget the Beatles. Their famous cut from the once counterculture Sgt. Pepper album "I Get By with a Little Help from My Friends" could be "I Get By with a Little Help from Depends."

The Who's great anthem about youth, "[Talkin' 'bout] My Generation," could now be "[Talkin' 'bout] My Medication." You get the idea.

Believe it or not, there are distinct advantages to being older. Have you ever met anyone over one hundred? I've had the chance to sit down with a number of these centenarians, and I appreciate their perspective. One reporter asked a 104-year-old woman, "What's the best thing about being 104?" The old lady thought about it for a moment and said, "There's no peer pressure."

~

*Most of us don't want to let people
know we're getting older.*

Most of us don't want to let people know we're getting older. But what's the problem with racking up some years? Hopefully you've learned a few things. Maybe you'll find yourself with a little hard-won wisdom to dispense. There's an old French proverb that says, "Forty is the old age of youth, and fifty is the youth of old age." If that's true, I'm definitely a young old person!

AS TIME GOES BY

Life is passing by…for all of us. Billy Graham was once asked what the greatest surprise of his life had been. His answer was, "The brevity of it."

I have to agree with him. I've been preaching for over thirty years now. I started when I was nineteen, and I'm fifty-two today. I remember so clearly when I first began speaking in meetings. Inevitably, someone would introduce me as a "young man," because I was usually way younger than everybody else. I never liked being singled out like that; it irritated me a little. Now if someone introduces me as a young man, I say, "Thank you!"

Here's what it comes down to. If you have placed your faith and trust in Jesus Christ as Savior, if you belong to Him, then you don't have to dread the passing of years. As Christians, we know the best is yet to come. As you walk day by day with the Lord, living the way He wants you to live, you will acquire experiences and memories, distilled truth that will be a blessing to you and others later in life, because you made the right choices and invested in the right things.

If you have put your faith in Jesus Christ, you need to know that He is with you right now, bringing His limitless power to bear on the details of your

If you have placed your faith in Jesus Christ, you don't have to dread the passing of years.

THE BEST IS YET TO COME

everyday life. His touch changes everything. And down the road? Well, there's nothing to stress about in our future—neither old age nor death nor the fresh new life that awaits just around the corner.

We can live that way—in a state of excited anticipation—knowing that when you're a believer, God saves the best for last.

In the second chapter of the book of John, Jesus performs a miracle that reminds us of both aspects of this encouraging truth: His power to transform our most impossible situations, and His promise of a future and a hope beyond our dreams and imagination.

THE LIFE OF THE PARTY

The next day Jesus' mother was a guest at a wedding celebration in the village of Cana in Galilee. Jesus and his disciples were also invited to the celebration. The wine supply ran out during the festivities, so Jesus' mother spoke to him about the problem. "They have no more wine," she told him.

"How does that concern you and me?" Jesus asked. "My time has not yet come."

But his mother told the servants, "Do whatever he tells you."

Six stone waterpots were standing there; they were used for Jewish ceremonial purposes and held twenty to thirty gallons each. Jesus told the servants, "Fill the jars with water." When the jars had been filled to the brim, he said, "Dip some out and take it to the master of ceremonies." So they followed his instructions.

When the master of ceremonies tasted the water that was now wine, not knowing where it had come from (though, of course, the servants knew), he called the bridegroom over. "Usually a host serves the best wine first," he said. "Then, when everyone is full and doesn't care, he brings out the less expensive wines. But you have kept the best until now!"

This miraculous sign at Cana in Galilee was Jesus' first display of his glory. And his disciples believed in him. (John 2:1–11, NLT)

Did it ever seem just a little strange to you that Jesus would pick a wedding as the place to launch His public ministry? Or that His first miracle would involve supplying refreshments at a wedding reception?

Doesn't it seem a little...random? Couldn't He have picked something just a bit more spectacular? If I had been the Lord's PR rep at the time, I probably would have counseled Him against embarking on His messianic career this way. I would have laid out a more "logical" strategy for Him.

I might have said, "Okay, Lord, as Your PR specialist, here's what I'm thinking. When it comes to miracles, I'd start right out with a big bang and heal a man born blind. Very dramatic. That will get You on the six o'clock news for sure. Or—better yet—cleanse a leper! That always goes over big. A real crowd pleaser. They love that. But then, if You *really* want to

~

Does it seem strange that Jesus picked a wedding as the place to launch His public ministry?

make a statement, raise someone from the dead. That would ice it; Your career would be off and running."

Jesus would say, "I was thinking about turning water into wine."

"What? Why would You even *want* to do a miracle like that? Where's the drama? Where's the news value?"

But that's just what He did. As the story opens in John 2, Jesus was attending a wedding, just kicking back and enjoying the celebration of a man and a woman committing themselves to each other in marriage.

Jesus, Creator of all, was the One who invented marriage. (Sadly, these days we have to add that there is only one marriage our Lord established and blesses—the union of a *man* and a *woman*.) It makes sense that He would join in the festivities and bless this young couple with His presence. A little known carpenter from Nazareth, He still had the cloak of relative anonymity as He feasted and celebrated this joyous occasion.

But water into wine? Why would the Messiah, the Son of God, begin His ministry with such an unusual act?

Let's think about it for a moment.

IF JESUS COULD DO THIS...

The Lord performed a miracle to bring happiness and joy to those celebrating the union of a man and a woman. And what Jesus did for this young couple at the wedding party in Cana shows that God can intervene in your life at any moment and provide you with exactly what you need. In fact, He may go far, far beyond your request to give you more than you ever thought to ask—or could have ever dreamed.

This wasn't some sleight of hand like dropping purple food dye into those huge thirty-gallon stone water vessels. Jesus created fine wine in an instant. This was wine that by every indication had come from premium grapes, grown on healthy vines, soaking in a long season of warm Middle East sunlight, then crushed in a winepress, stored in special skins or casks, and aged to absolute perfection.

I know there are people out there who consider themselves wine connoisseurs (I don't happen to be one of them). But if you happen to be channel surfing and touch down on the food channel for a few minutes, you might see some guy taking tiny sips out of a wineglass, swirling it around, and exclaiming about its qualities. He will tell you more than you ever wanted to know about all the complex subtleties of its aroma, its bouquet, its "finish," and on and on. For some people (sometimes referred to as "wine snobs"), this is an elaborate science.

And Jesus created 180 gallons of superlative wine in the blink of an eye. If He had chosen to do so, of course, He could have turned the whole Sea of Galilee into cabernet. (He once turned the mighty Nile River into blood.) But He limited the miracle to those six stone waterpots at a wedding feast in the little back-water town of Cana.

If Jesus could do this—if He could take generic well water and completely change its molecular structure in the space of a heartbeat, making it into wine so wonderful that it startled and amazed an experienced connoisseur…if Jesus could pull this off—then what situation in your life could possibly be too complex or overwhelming for Him? What challenge in your life could possibly exceed *this* one?

Sometimes we find ourselves in some tangled combination of distressing circumstances, feel like we're in way over our heads, and try to explain it all to the Lord, hoping He will somehow understand all of the complicating factors we barely comprehend ourselves.

Not to worry. Jesus grasps your situation in greater depth and detail than you could achieve in a million years of stressing about it. This miracle in the second chapter of John, our Lord's first supernatural act, proves He is the Master of every imaginable situation, right down to the most subtle, seemingly insignificant details. Through this miracle, Jesus showed He had at His immediate disposal unlimited power to do anything He chose to do.

You may not need to have your tap water turned into wine, but understanding and tapping into your Lord's limitless strength and wisdom could be very important...when the doctor calls you into his office, sits you down, and tells you that you have inoperable cancer...or when the boss pulls you aside and says, "I'm sorry, but we have to let you go"...or when that unexpected bill comes...or when your spouse tells you he or she wants out of your marriage...or when your child gets in trouble with the law...or when you're slapped with an unexpected lawsuit.

It's good—very, very good—to know that none of these things catch God by surprise, and nothing limits His ability to intervene in our lives, to absolutely transform the most snarled, knotted, and convoluted situations, and to accomplish things beyond our conception.

Now glory be to God! By his mighty power at work within us, he is able to accomplish infinitely more than we would ever dare to ask or hope. (Ephesians 3:20, NLT)

NOW OR NEVER?

Jesus had said, "Fill the waterpots," and the servants did their part. There is always a part for God to play and a part for us to play.

As the water was distributed, of course, it turned into wine. The man in charge of the feast knew something extraordinary was up after one sip. I can almost see the surprise and wonder light up his face. Where had these kids come up with a vintage like this one? Undoubtedly, this was the best wine he had ever tasted—or would ever taste again.

And then a look of puzzlement must have washed over his features. He called out to the bridegroom, "Usually a host serves the best wine first.... Then, when everyone is full and doesn't care, he brings out the less expensive wines. But you have kept the best until now!" (John 2:10, NLT).

God always saves the best for last. That's His way, that's His plan.

Not so with Satan. His motto is: *Grab for the best right now, while you can get it. Who knows what's to come?* The devil likes to bring out all his big guns up front. He offers his most enticing, appealing stuff in the beginning, especially when you are young. It's amazing how many young men and women—with their whole futures and potential before them—ravage and destroy their lives with drugs, alcohol, and a life of immorality. And yet every new generation of

~

God always saves the best for last. That's His way, that's His plan.

young people that comes along acts like they were the ones who discovered this stuff.

The devil is very good at packaging his wares. Madison Avenue has nothing on hell; the evil one can make very bad merchandise look really cool. He slides it in front of you and says, "Hey, you've got to do this. You have to try this for yourself. Don't listen to what your parents are saying." He knows how to make these ventures off the straight path seem very attractive and appealing. After all, he's had about six thousand years to practice on men and women and hone his techniques. And at the same time, He can take things of infinite, eternal value and wrap them in old newspaper, making them look really lame.

When Eve was in the garden and saw that forbidden fruit, she was strongly attracted to it. When I think of that scene, I certainly don't think of the traditional depiction of an "apple." (Where do people get this apple stuff? It wasn't an apple growing on that tree.) Personally, I think of a red-gold peach, dead ripe, almost glowing in the sunset, full of juice and ready to fall off the branch right into your hand. Frankly, an apple wouldn't have attracted me at all. I can take or leave an apple. Mmm, but a sweet, plump peach? I can see that. It had to look good because the Bible says it was pleasant to the eyes.

The devil will say, "Try this."

And it looks good at first. It really does. And that first taste—it's exciting. But then, later…well, it's a different story.

Right about this moment I'm thinking of a famous doughnut chain. These are folks who make doughnuts that melt in your mouth like manna. You pull into the parking lot early in the morning when you see the "Hot" sign first light up. You want the doughnuts fresh. For me personally, it's all about the glazed doughnuts. When these celebrated doughnuts are cold, they're just ordinary mortal confections. But when they're coming down that conveyor belt, hot from the deep fryer, glistening with glaze…aaah, that's as close as you'll get to the bread of angels right there. To take it to the next level, of course, you need some ice-cold milk. I think the most I've eaten is five doughnuts in one sitting.

Oh, they're so great going down. But about ten minutes later, you hate life. You take a major sugar hit, and your temporary high quickly gives way to a crushing depression. And on top of that, you've got this big glob of greasy dough sitting in your stomach. Then, of course, if you make this a regular habit, your pants won't fit anymore.

Sin can be that way. You say, "Forget tomorrow. Forget this best-is-yet-to-come stuff. I'm going to grab my fun right now." And the first time *is* fun. The experience looks really good rolling off that conveyor belt. The second time it's still a rush. The third time you begin to feel the effects…and it's not so much fun anymore. An hour later, you're saying, *What was I thinking? Why did I do that? This is horrible.* That's about the time guilt and regret kick in, and you begin to understand the repercussions of what you've done.

Yes, the devil will always offer appealing stuff up front, because he knows how to do it and knows what works. But the price is always, always too expensive. Don't take his bait!

Why? Because time will pass. The years will slip by. Before you know it, you'll have more years behind you than in front of you…and you will find yourself looking back. And those times will be unbelievably desolate and empty if you have followed the ways of Satan and the flesh.

WHAT HAVE I (REALLY) MISSED?

It's amazing to me that even though I'm in my fifties, I still encounter people I went to high school with here in Southern California. Here and there, maybe at a mall, maybe on the beach, I'll run into people I knew from those years. It only takes a minute or two to see the course their life has taken, and the sadness they now live with every day of their lives.

I gave my life to Christ at seventeen. Did I miss anything? Well, yes, I suppose I did. I missed a lot of parties. I missed a lot of experiences. I missed a lot of things that other kids my age were into. But now, when thirty-plus years have gone by, and I look at what it has done to them…some of them into their fourth, fifth marriages, some of them still addicted, still living the party lifestyle, others just wandering through an empty, futile life, I look at them and say, "Have I really missed anything?"

For me, life has only gotten better. Not necessarily

*As the years go by and the experiences build,
you begin reaping what you have sown.*

easier, or less complicated, or less pressured, or more trouble-free, but *better*. Sweeter. Richer. Deeper. More satisfying.

Every day, every month, every year of walking with Jesus Christ just gets better and better.

You might say, "Greg, that's a nice, pleasant message to preach at a retirement center, but what's it got to do with me?" The truth is, it's an even more important message for younger people. Why? Because you determine the end of your life at the beginning of it. You decide where you're going to be twenty years from now *today* by what choices you make and what roads you take.

Are you at a crossroads in life right now?

God says, "I have set before you life and death, blessings and curses. Now choose life, so that you and your children may live" (Deuteronomy 30:19, NIV).

As the years go by and the experiences build, you

begin reaping what you have sown. Those proverbial chickens come home to roost, just as they always will. The Bible says, "Do not be deceived, God is not mocked; for whatever a man sows, that he will also reap. For he who sows to his flesh will of the flesh reap corruption, but he who sows to the Spirit will of the Spirit reap everlasting life" (Galatians 6:7–8).

Here's the choice. You can either reap the bitter repercussions of living sinfully, or you can enjoy the sweet fruit of a godly life.

Every day, from the time you rise in the morning, you will be either sowing to the flesh or sowing to the Spirit. By that I mean you are either building yourself up spiritually and getting closer to God, or you are neglecting spiritual things and going after whatever draws you in at the moment, living for your own impulses, whims, and desires.

That is a choice each of us must make. There is no "third option."

If you are a Christian, you know the best is yet to come in life. The best is yet to come in your growth as a person who walks with God and becomes more like Jesus day by day. Yes, we Christians have the same

health problems and aches and pains as we age as anyone else. But we know that there is more to life than
just this body. We know that there is life with a capital "L" on the other side, when we enter into God's
presence. Indeed, the best is yet to come.

If you're not a Christian, the *worst* is yet to come.
I don't care how much fun you may be having at the
moment, or what great experiences you're piling up at
this time. The worst is yet to come, because the Bible
says there will be a reaping of what you sow. Scripture
tells us of a future judgment, where you will be held
accountable for how you lived your life and—most
important—what you did with Jesus Christ.

The miracle at the wedding in Cana happened
because Jesus was *invited*. They invited Him into their
home, they invited Him to their wedding, they invited
Him to share in their joy, and guess what? He came.
He showed up at the party. And because He was there,
He changed an embarrassing shortfall into a miracle
of provision. He stepped into an impossible situation
and transformed it in a way no one could have
guessed or predicted.

He's still in the business of doing that very thing.

But He'll never just barge into your life—into your worries and fears and sorrows—uninvited. He waits to be asked. Once you do, once you invite Him to join the party, you have absolutely no idea of the difference He can make in your today.

And tomorrow? Well, I'll just say it again.

The best is yet to come.

BELIEVING IS SEEING

NOT LONG AGO, I WOKE UP EARLY ON A SATURDAY morning and walked by my eighteen-year-old son Jonathan's room.

His bedroom door was open, and when I glanced inside, I saw that his bed was made and he was gone. I just stood there a moment, trying to process what I was seeing. And then I panicked, a sick feeling sweeping through me. *Where is he? What happened to him? Did he not come home last night? I should have waited up for him!* I went down the hall to his brother's room and woke him up.

"Christopher! Where's Jonathan?"

"I dunno, Dad," he mumbled. "I didn't see his car last night."

So he hadn't come home! Had he been in an accident? Was he a victim of foul play? Was he lying in some hospital somewhere—or worse?

And then the thought crossed my mind, *Maybe he stayed all night at his friend's house.* So I called the friend's number, got somebody out of bed, and...sure enough, that's where he was. My wife had simply forgotten to tell me. But I had immediately thought the worst, and found myself overcome with fear.

Here's the problem with fear. It likes to hang around with a companion known as worry. Fear and worry work in tandem, like Batman and Robin. And before you know it, you find yourself caught up in a horrible game of "What if?" These are two very powerful emotions.

Worry is one of the most destructive forces a per-

~

Fear likes to hang around with a companion known as worry.

son can experience. Modern medical research has shown that worry breaks down our resistance to disease. More than that, it can actually *create* diseases of the nervous system, the digestive organs, and the heart. It's been said that excessive worry can literally shorten human life.

Isn't that ironic? Because one of the very things we may be worrying about is how long we will live!

A number of years ago I remember watching a local TV news program, and they kept teasing the audience with an upcoming piece about a hundred-year-old man who was going to give his secret to long life. Well, I was curious (just as they intended) and stayed around until the end of the broadcast where they showed the brief interview with this old gentleman.

What a letdown!

The interviewers asked him, "What's your secret to living so long?" His answer was rather unexpected, to say the least.

"Well, sir," he rasped, "every day I eat a hot dog."

A hot dog? That was it? You would have thought he'd say something like, "I've always been a vegetarian," or "I'm really careful to exercise." But no. Every day of his life he downs a greasy dog smeared with mustard and relish. And they showed the kind of hot dogs he ate. They weren't the fancy kosher ones, made out of lean beef; they were the cheapest kind you can buy—the ones with rat tails and who knows what else ground up in them. I couldn't believe it. The fountain of youth is a cheap frankfurter?

But the fact is, there are worse things you can do to your health than eating store-brand hot dogs! A life filled with anxiety and worry can slice years off your life, and life off your years. The very word *worry* comes from an old English term that means "to choke." And that's exactly what it will do when it intrudes in our lives.

THE SECOND SIGN

In the last chapter, we read about our Lord's first miracle at the wedding in Cana of Galilee. Two chapters later in the same Gospel, John tells the story of a very worried man—a man filled with panic and anxiety—who came to Jesus in an hour of crushing need.

He had good reason to be afraid; his dearly loved

son was at home with a high fever, near death. But somehow he'd heard that Jesus of Nazareth was in the area, and so leaving his son's bedside, the distraught man hurried out to seek the mysterious rabbi everyone had been talking about.

So Jesus came again to Cana of Galilee where He had made the water wine. And there was a certain nobleman whose son was sick at Capernaum. When he heard that Jesus had come out of Judea into Galilee, he went to Him and implored Him to come down and heal his son, for he was at the point of death. Then Jesus said to him, "Unless you people see signs and wonders, you will by no means believe."

The nobleman said to Him, "Sir, come down before my child dies!"

Jesus said to him, "Go your way; your son lives." So the man believed the word that Jesus spoke to him, and he went his way. And as he was now going down, his servants met him and told him, saying, "Your son lives!"

Then he inquired of them the hour when he got better. And they said to him, "Yesterday at the seventh hour the fever left him." So the father knew that it was at the same hour in which Jesus said to him, "Your son lives." And he himself believed, and his whole household.

This again is the second sign Jesus did when He had come out of Judea into Galilee. (John 4:46–54)

Notice that John identifies these two miracles—the water into wine and the healing of the nobleman's son—as *signs*. In other words, these are pictures that do more than simply record an event…they also point to a deeper truth.

What do these demonstrations of the Lord's power have in common? In both cases, in both signs, people believed. After Jesus turned the water into wine we read that His disciples believed. In the second sign, the healing of the government official's son, we read that this man and his family believed. Both of these miracles brought belief.

Now what's different about the two miracles?

~

*Into each of our lives come days of gladness and laughter,
and also gut-wrenching anxiety and grief.*

Jesus' first sign came at a wedding—a festive scene of celebration. And the second miracle, the healing, impacted a scene of sickness, desperation, great anxiety, and the shadow of death. One was a picture of joy, the other a picture of sorrow.

Life is filled with both, isn't it? Into each of our lives come days of gladness and laughter, and also gut-wrenching anxiety and grief.

By placing these miracles side by side, John shows us our Lord's sufficiency to meet our needs *no matter what we are facing.* As one commentator put it, "Jesus is more than equal to either occasion. He has a place in all circumstances. If we invite Him into our times of innocent happiness He will increase our joy. If we call on Him in times of sorrow, anxiety or bereavement, He can bring consolation, comfort and a joy that is not of this world."[1]

So maybe you find yourself with a light heart

today, in a sun-splashed season of happiness. Savor it. Enjoy it. Bask in it. It's from the hand of God, but it won't last forever. Then again, maybe you're enduring some terribly difficult days right now. Get through them. Cling to the Lord Jesus. Hold on to your faith, and take your stand on God's good promises. The dark time won't last forever, either.

But here's the great good news. Whatever your situation, Jesus is there for you. To share your joy and enter into your times of celebration, as He did in the miracle at Cana, and also to comfort and strengthen you in your time of fear and sorrow, as He was doing with this troubled man. Whatever your "right now" need might be, He is God of the now. And around every bend of life in the years God allows to you…the best is yet to come.

∼

Whatever your "right now" need might be
He is God of the now.

A WORRIED MAN

Now who was this man who came to Jesus? John identifies him as a royal official or a king's man—part of the court of Herod, possibly a member of the royal family. We can safely conclude that he was a man of substantial wealth, as Herod's men were apt to be. He was an individual who by anyone's standards had everything one could possibly want in life.

Everything but peace of mind.

His child had contracted a fever, and this loving father had to stand helplessly by as that precious life just drained away before his eyes. And now his son was on the verge of death.

As a pastor making hospital calls, I have been with many people near death. It's a challenging aspect of any shepherd's job. But the most difficult part of all is when you see a child suffer. Performing a funeral service for a child is one of the hardest things I've ever had to do. Because no parent wants to outlive their children.

And here was a man who dearly loved his son, and knew that his boy's life hung by a thread. There was nothing that all of this nobleman's power, wealth, and prestige could do about it. He might have had all the most enviable connections to Herod's palace and the Roman governor, but the only connection that mattered on that day was his connection with the God of heaven. So, he wisely went to Jesus.

Sometimes people imagine that money could solve all their problems. *O God, if I could just win the lotto. I would tithe! I would support missionaries! If only the Publishers Clearing House van would stop in front of my front door, my worries would be over.* It's not true of course. Yes, money can alleviate certain problems. But it can also create even deeper problems than it solves.

CAN'T BUY ME LOVE

In an interview, actor Sylvester Stallone talked about the impact money has had on his life. Here's a famous celebrity with a number of commercially successful movies and a hit television program to his credit, and a man who has made a great deal of money. Yet Stallone told the interviewer, "Money does not bring peace of mind. Actually money brings about more problems. Everything is magnified a hundred thousand times. That's not to complain, but once you make a fortune you think it all becomes green lights and blue skies, and it's not true. As a matter of fact," said Stallone, "it brings out some of the most vile characteristics of other people's personalities that you can imagine."

This royal official from Capernaum had plenty of wealth and financial security, but those things couldn't help him in his day of trouble. There are many, many things that money cannot buy. As the Beatles sang, "Money can't buy me love."

And there are other things that money can't buy you. Money can buy you a king-sized bed, but it can't buy you a good night's sleep. Money can buy you a giant house, but it can't buy you a home. Money can buy you a companion for the night, but it can't buy you a friend. And as we see in this account in the Gospel of John, money can't buy you life and health, either.

The shadow of trouble and sorrow had fallen over this man's home…as it will fall over everyone's home sooner or later. It's not *if* it will happen, it's *when*. And this man didn't know what to do, didn't know where to turn. But then he got word that this remarkable teacher, Jesus of Nazareth, was about 17 miles away from Capernaum, and he knew he had to find Him as quickly as possible. I think we can safely assume that he rode the fastest stallion in his stable. It's worth noting that he didn't get someone to go in his stead. He himself went to the Lord with the most urgent request of his life.

> When he heard that Jesus had come out of Judea into Galilee, he went to Him and implored Him to come down and heal his son, for he was at the point of death. (v. 47)

Imagine the scene. Jesus moved along the street with that ever-present crowd thronging Him. And suddenly this nobleman thundered onto the scene on a beautiful stallion. Dressed in the royal finery of his day, he would have certainly turned heads.

Quickly dismounting, he ran over to Jesus. And the word that is translated "implored" means that he begged Him. He pleaded with Jesus for the life of his boy.

"Lord, please, I beg You, I'm calling on You, please touch my dear son. My boy that I love is dying. Sir, please do something."

In that moment, I think the last thing that nobleman cared about was his image. He didn't care about how it looked as he begged Jesus for help. He didn't care what anybody thought. He didn't care that he was down on his knees in the dust in all that finery. He didn't care if it seemed proper or seemly or dignified. All he cared about was his boy.

NOT THE ANSWER WE EXPECTED

Now one of the things this royal official—and all the rest of us—have to learn about prayer is that while God answers all prayer, He doesn't always answer it in the way we want or expect. And our faith must be deep enough and wide enough to embrace and encompass the answer God gives us in whatever way He chooses to give it.

~

Jesus wanted to save a man's eternal soul.

Jesus was willing to heal this man's son, but didn't say so right away. Why? Because He wanted to draw something greater out of that situation than merely healing a boy of physical illness.

He wanted to save a man's eternal soul.

And that just happens to be the happy ending to this story. The nobleman and his family came to faith in Jesus. Though it may not seem like it at the time, there are some things more important than getting your bills paid or your health restored or resolving whatever crisis you might be facing at the moment. The most crucial thing in all of life is to come into right relationship with Jesus Christ. No other priority even comes close. And sometimes God will allow calamity or hardship to get your attention, to wake you up to your need for a Savior.

C. S. Lewis wrote in *The Problem of Pain* that God whispers to us in our pleasures, speaks to us in our conscience, but shouts in our pain. He declared pain

"God's megaphone to rouse a deaf world."[2] Sometimes God whispers and we don't pay attention. Sometimes God speaks and we don't respond. He rings our number and we don't pick up. So He gets out that megaphone of pain, and boy, does that wake us up quickly.

That's what's happening to the dad in this story. He's in great pain, and he calls on Jesus. He pleads for an answer, but the Lord's reply seems surprisingly blunt and abrupt.

> Then Jesus said to him, "Unless you people see signs and wonders, you will by no means believe." (v. 48)

Ouch! Isn't that a tad harsh? Maybe a little cold-hearted? What kind of thing is that to say to a man in such obvious anguish? It's as if Jesus throws a cup of cold water right in his face. How could the Lord be so detached and unsympathetic?

Actually, that's not the case at all. A closer look reveals something different altogether. Jesus was not demeaning or insulting this man. He was using this as a teaching moment to bring him forward spiritually. First of all, when Jesus said, "Unless you people see signs and wonders," it was in the plural. He was using that encounter as an opportunity to address the crowd. So Jesus was essentially saying to the people all around Him, "You know, the problem here is that all you people care about is the razzle-dazzle of miracles, and you have no interest in God Himself."

But I love this nobleman, on his knees before Jesus. He wouldn't give up. He refused to be discouraged or deterred. He just kept pressing on, pressing in, imploring and begging the Lord.

Do you have a big problem on your heart right now? Maybe you don't know where to turn or what to do. You wake up at three o'clock in the morning, and as soon as you open your eyes you're filled with worry. Have you ever had that happen? You start thinking...*Oh no, what if this happens? What will I do?* And then you're wide awake, and can't go back to sleep and get your rest.

Let me make a suggestion. The next time that happens, the next time you wake up and worry comes knocking at the door, send the Lord to answer it. Say to Him, "Lord, I commit this thing to You. I have no ability to fix it, especially at three o'clock in the morning, so I'm just leaving it in Your hands, and I'm going back to sleep. See You in the morning, Lord." That's not a cop-out. That's a person who understands the power of prayer. That's a person who trusts in the Lord with all his heart, and leans not on his own understanding, as it says in Proverbs 3:5–6.

Notice how Jesus replied to the nobleman in verse 50. He said, "Go your way; your son lives." Jesus had put a test in front of this man and he passed it. The Lord's first response had seemed to be turning the sorrowing dad away, but in reality He was drawing him out. He was saying, "Son, I will do what you ask, but I want to see you be persistent. I want to see you hang in there with Me."

Maybe as you read these words you're facing your own crisis, your own "dark night of the soul." And

~

The next time you wake up and worry comes knocking at the door, send the Lord to answer it.

you've been calling on the Lord, but haven't gotten an answer in the affirmative. Don't give up. Keep praying. Follow the example of the man in this story.

Finally Jesus said the words this worried dad longed with all his heart to hear: "Go your way; your son lives." A more accurate translation would be, "You may go. Your son is living. *He lives right now.*" Notice that in these words Jesus both answers the father's prayer and denies it at the same time. The nobleman had not only prayed for his son to be healed, but he unwittingly attempted to dictate the terms of that healing. While I don't think he meant to press specific demands on Jesus, the implication was clear: "Lord, I know I live seventeen miles away and I know You are busy...but please, You need to come with me back to my house to see my boy. I implore You, Lord."

But the Lord basically replied to him, "No, I'm not returning to your house with you. I don't need to. Your son is fine. I give you My word." That was all this man had...the word of Jesus. And that was all he needed.

Some people like to say, "Seeing is believing." Jesus would say, "Believing is seeing." Look at verse

50. "So the man believed the word that Jesus spoke to him, and he went his way."

He had faith, because faith sees the unseen. On the basis of Jesus' words (and with no cell phone to call and double-check), this nobleman saw his son healthy and well. Not only did he believe it, he put shoe leather to it. He turned on his heel without another word and walked away.

Hebrews 11:1 says, "What is faith? It is the confident assurance that what we hope for is going to happen. It is the evidence of things we cannot yet see" (NLT).

TAKING HIS TIME

Now here's an interesting twist in the story. Look at verses 51 and 52 of John 4. "As he was going down, his servants met him and told him, saying, 'Your son lives!' Then he inquired of them the hour when he got better. And they said to him, 'Yesterday at the seventh hour the fever left him.'"

Notice the word *yesterday.*

In other words, the nobleman went home *the next*

day. Here's what happened. Once Jesus had pronounced his son alive and healed, he decided to hang out in Cana for the night. If it were me, I would have jumped on that horse and galloped back home as fast as I could go. If I rode extra hard, I might have made it home for dinner. But surprisingly, this once-distraught official stayed overnight in town. He left for home the next day, and the servants met him on the way to tell him the good news he already knew.

This amazes me! It's as though the man thought, *Well, why rush home? The boy is fine, and I have the Master's word on it. And hey, how often do I get to Cana? Besides, there's a great seafood restaurant in town I've been wanting to try. Why not? Jesus said everything was good at home.* This to me is a great declaration of real faith in this father's life.

So the servants met him with the glorious news, and he asked them, "When did it happen?" They told him it happened at one o'clock in the afternoon. I can just see the official nodding his head, a big smile spreading across his face. Because he had marked the time when Jesus said, "Your son is healed." He looked at his little sundial on his wrist and said to himself,

~

The difference is faith, believing that Jesus is able and willing to do what He has promised.

"Okay, it's one o'clock. Tomorrow, I will ask my servants what time the boy was made well." And when the servants confirmed the exact time, his faith and joy just soared.

How different this nobleman's ride out and ride back must have been. On his way to find Jesus, he would have been breathless, his heart pounding. But now he rides home in a leisurely manner after spending the night in the Cana Hilton. His anxiety has melted away like a bad dream. And the difference is faith, believing that Jesus is able and willing to do what He has promised. With a touch? Not even that. With only a word.

GETTING YOUR FAITH IN GEAR

So what do we learn in this story about our own lives? *We learn that when crisis hits we must run to Jesus.*

Peter tells us to "cast all your anxiety on him because he cares for you" (1 Peter 5:7, NIV). Don't back off. Don't let up. Keep praying. Keep bringing your need to the Lord. Keep releasing your cares and anxieties to Him, even if you have to do it every other minute through your day.

Do you have a crisis right now? Bring it to Jesus Christ. He has asked you to do so. Even more, He has *commanded* you to do so.

What else do we learn? *Don't tell God how to answer, but simply trust Him.* Jesus didn't do everything the official requested that day; it didn't fall into place in just the way this anxious dad thought it would. But he put his trust in Jesus anyway...and the result was all he wanted. We must do the same. There are times when God allows things to happen in our lives that make no logical sense at all, but it is then that we must learn to trust Him, knowing that He will finish what He has begun. God doesn't do things in a halfway manner.

Many of us have faith, but don't use it. And if you don't use it, it doesn't do much good in your daily life.

A lot of people in Southern California drive SUVs

these days. And when you're shopping for an SUV, you want to know about its four-wheel-drive capabilities. You say to the salesman, okay, tell me what this thing can do. And you look at all these cool pictures of your dream machine climbing up mountains at a forty-five-degree angle, or blasting through the mud, or crossing some river with water up to the windows.

"Great," you say, "I'll take it." And you buy some cool accessories and set it up to look really gnarly, like it's ready for the mountains on the back side of the moon.

But do you ever take it into the dirt? Are you kidding? (Do you know what I paid for this thing?) You stay on asphalt for the life of the car, and take it through the carwash twice a week to keep it spotless and gleaming. You have the *capacity* for serious off-road four-wheeling, but you never let those knobby tires ever touch gravel. It's enough to know that the capacity is there if you ever wanted it (which most of us here in Southern California never do).

We can be that way with our faith. We imagine that we're loaded up with it…we talk about being strong in our faith…but we never want to use it. It never gets out of the garage and into the world. God wants to grow a faith in us that is active and strong and ready for those inevitable tests and trials of life.

One final thing we learn from this account. *We must accept God's Word to us by faith and not allow ourselves to be overcome by worry and fear.* The nobleman was in one of the most trying circumstances a parent can ever face. But he chose to put his full faith in the Word of Jesus.

Do you believe God's Word to you? God has spoken to you in the pages of the Bible. He has given you promises—thousands and thousands of promises that you can take to the bank. But you won't experience any benefit in your life unless you take the time to read the Scripture, memorize some of those promises of God, and then put them into action.

Maybe God is using a set of circumstances in your life to bring you to a place of faith, to bring you to a

~

We imagine that we're loaded up with it . . . we talk about being strong in our faith . . . but we never want to use it.

place of commitment so you would call upon Him and lean your full weight upon Him. You might say, "Well, Greg, it's hard for me to believe. I need some proof. You have to show me that God is real. Show me and I will believe."

Essentially Jesus would say, "Believe and I will show you." No, seeing is not believing. *Believing is seeing.* And if you would just take a little step of faith, you would see what God could do for you as well.

THREE

DON'T
WORRY...PRAY!

WE LIVE IN FRIGHTENING TIMES.

Besides all the normal fears about our future, our employment, our health, and our children, there are the added fears of terrorism in this post-9/11 world in which we live.

There is certainly reason for concern.

But there is no reason to worry.

I want to make that distinction. To be concerned about an issue means you are aware, informed, and alert. Worrying is different. It's not only a highly unproductive activity, it is also a *faithless* activity that has no part in the life of a believer. Rather than improving your situation—any situation—worry brings paralysis and eventual apathy at the very time when you need your personal and divine resources the most. When you worry about the future, you cripple your ability to think, act, and exercise faith in the present.

We're all aware that every day has its own quota of problems. That was our Lord's clear message in the Sermon on the Mount. "So don't worry about tomorrow, for tomorrow will bring its own worries. Today's trouble is enough for today" (Matthew 6:34, NLT).

Some of our problems are constant, day-to-day challenges. Others come and go. When you get up in the morning, you'll have your daily allotment of heartaches, adversities, disappointments, difficulties…and a sprinkling of potential impossibilities.

What you *don't* want to do is go after tomorrow's quota as well. In other words, you don't want to start

～

Some of our problems are constant,
day-to-day challenges.

stressing about things that haven't even happened (and may never happen).

Worrying does not empty tomorrow of its sorrow. It empties today of its strength.

God will give you the strength to face each day with enough grace to manage. Whatever you may face, He will not abandon you in your hour of need. But if you worry about it, you will only compound your troubles.

There's an old fable about Death walking toward a town one morning. A man stops Death and says, "What are you intending to do?"

"I plan on taking one hundred people," Death replies.

"That's horrible!"

"That's what I do. It's just the way it is."

The man hurried ahead of Death into town to warn everyone of what was coming.

When evening fell he met Death again. The man protested, "You told me you were going to take a hundred people. Why did a *thousand* die?"

"I kept my word," Death responded. "I took only a hundred people. Worry took the others."

Many of the people in hospital beds today in America are constant worriers. Forty-three percent of all adults suffer health effects due to worry and stress. We're told that 79 to 90 percent of all visits to primary care physicians are stress-related complaints or disorders. We are a culture in the unrelenting grip of anxiety and worry. You could write on countless American gravestones the epitaph "Hurried, Worried, Buried."

NO WORRIES?

Maybe you ought to consider hiring someone to worry for you. I heard the story of the man who was known to be a real worrywart, always fretting about something. One day his close friend was surprised to see him looking completely relaxed and at ease, seemingly without a care in the world.

The friend said, "You don't seem to be uptight today."

"I haven't worried for a good month," the man replied with a smile.

"Really. Why?"

"Simple. I hired someone to worry for me."

"You—what? Where did you find somebody like that?"

"I took an ad out in the paper."

"You did? What did the ad say?"

"It said, 'I will pay you one thousand dollars a day if you come and worry for me.'"

"A thousand dollars a day? You don't make anything close to that kind of money. How do you intend to pay this guy?"

"That's for him to worry about."

When we held a Harvest Crusade in Australia several years ago, I couldn't help noticing a popular Aussie expression. If you ask for directions or place an order in a restaurant and then say thank you, they will reply, "No worries, mate." I like that! Not only is it a pleasant reply, it's theologically sound. Most of the stuff we worry about never happens anyway.

Dr. Walter Caver reported a survey on worry that indicated only 8 percent of the things people worried about were legitimate matters of concern. The other 92 percent were imaginary, involving either matters that had almost no possibility of happening, or things over which a person had no control anyway.

I heard about a woman who worried for forty years that she would die of cancer, but ended up dying of pneumonia at the age of seventy. When you think about it, she wasted forty years worrying about the wrong thing!

Then there are people who always seem so worried about what others think of them. It's been said that you wouldn't worry so much about what people think about you…if you knew how seldom they do!

Worry never helps, it only hurts.

Does that mean we don't have concerns? That we hide our heads in the sand, and close our eyes to what's going on around us? Not at all. I'm simply saying worry itself is counterproductive.

God gives us some practical information in Philippians 4 that tells us what we should do *instead* of worrying. It gives us three principles that, if

~

Most of the stuff we worry about never happens anyway.

applied, would help us banish worry from our thoughts.

PAUL'S PRESCRIPTION

I'll make a confession here: By nature, I'm something of a worrier myself, and have a tendency to fret. Words like these from the pen of the apostle Paul are of particular comfort to me.

> Rejoice in the Lord always. Again I will say, rejoice! Let your gentleness be known to all men. The Lord is at hand. Be anxious for nothing, but in everything by prayer and supplication, with thanksgiving, let your requests be made known to God; and the peace of God, which surpasses all understanding, will guard your hearts and minds through Christ Jesus.
>
> Finally, brethren, whatever things are true, whatever things are noble, whatever things are just, whatever things are pure, whatever things are lovely, whatever things are of good report,

if there is any virtue and if there is anything praiseworthy—meditate on these things. The things which you learned and received and heard and saw in me, these do, and the God of peace will be with you. (Philippians 4:4–9)

Where was Paul when he wrote these words?

That's a significant question. If we learn that Paul was kicked back in a lawn chair in the sunshine on the island of Crete, sipping an iced tea, we might say, "It's easy for him to tell us, 'Don't worry,' because he's living the good life." But the fact is, when Paul wrote these words he was in dire straits.

It had been Paul's desire for years to take the gospel to Rome. God certainly fulfilled his dream, but the apostle probably had no idea that he would arrive in Rome in chains, as a prisoner. Locked up, he awaited an unknown fate. He knew that the sound of every footstep outside his door might be the executioner, taking him away to behead him. Then again, it might be the jailer with an acquittal order in his hand, setting him free. He just didn't know.

It was a pathetic, miserable situation he found

himself in. Yet at this very time in this very place, he is able to say, "Rejoice in the Lord always. Again I will say, rejoice!"

Paul faced uncertainty—about his very life. As Americans, we too face uncertainty as a nation right now. We hope that the war on terrorism will come to a quick conclusion, and yet we know it might drag on for years. We hope the bad guys don't gain access to weapons of mass destruction, but we really have no idea. We look at North Korea, Iran, and China, and wonder if we might one day be locked in conflict with one of these nuclear nations.

We look at all of the problems that life brings us. We wonder how long we will live, or how we'll get through a particular situation or dilemma we may be facing.

Paul—who by all logic ought to have been worried—wasn't worried. In the original language, "Rejoice in the Lord always" is not a suggestion, but

~

We look at all of the problems that life brings us.

rather a *command.* In other words, God commands you as a Christian to rejoice. To disobey this directive is no better than disobeying any other command of God.

In spite of whatever you may be wrestling with right now, remember that God is still on the throne. He still loves you. His plans for you are still good. He will never leave you or forsake you.

Let's consider three practical steps Paul gives us for banishing worry from our lives.

1. RIGHT PRAYING

In everything by prayer and supplication, with thanksgiving, let your requests be made known to God. (v. 6)

Notice that Paul says "in *everything* by prayer."

He doesn't say "in some things by prayer" or "in only the really big things by prayer." This reminds us that nothing is too big or too small to bring to our God. He is interested in even the smallest of details.

The next time you feel an inclination to worry,

quickly switch mental gears and pray *instead*. We need to form the habit of turning to God when we feel worry approaching. Your reaction in times of trouble should be like a conditioned reflex.

Our body experiences both normal and conditioned reflexes. A normal reflex isn't taught; it's automatic. If I reach out and touch a hot iron, I pull my hand back. I didn't have to teach myself to do that. I automatically pull away from something that causes pain. Even a small baby would pull his hand away from something hot.

It reminds me of a story of the guy who went to a doctor with two severely burned ears. "This is horrible," the doctor said. "How did you burn both of your ears?"

The man said, "I was doing some ironing. The phone rang. I got a little confused and I answered the iron instead of the phone."

The doctor winced. "That's awful," he said, "But how did you burn the other ear?"

"He called back."

It's an automatic reflex for (most) people to pull away something that would burn them. But at the same time, our behavior and responses are also governed by *conditioned* reflexes. Sometimes in our church we will sing "God Bless America." And everyone stands up. Why? Nobody up front says, "All right, this is a patriotic song, everybody stand." And yet everyone does. It's a conditioned reflex. You just know this is a song to stand up to. You get to your feet in honor of an anthem like this, out of a sense of love for country.

When you were learning to drive you had to consciously think about everything you did. Remember? "Okay, I'm coming to a stoplight, *step on the brake.* All right, I've got a turn coming up. *Signal.*" Now when you drive, do you still think about it? Of course not. When I first started driving I had a little Chevy Corvair with a manual transmission. I had to learn how to drive that stick shift, and sometimes I would get confused and stomp on the brake instead of the clutch. But after you drive and drive and drive some more, you train yourself and develop conditioned reflexes.

So what happens to you when worry comes into your mind? Oftentimes, our natural tendency is to embrace it. To hold on to those worrisome thoughts, turning them over and over, until our whole body becomes stressed. And once you get into that uptight frame of mind, you think of even *more* stuff to worry about. It comes down on you like one of those heavy lead aprons the dentist lays over your chest before he x-rays your teeth.

By developing a *conditioned* reflex, however, you can change those knee-jerk tendencies to lapse into anxiety. Let's say an unpleasant thought suddenly pops into your mind, and you think, "Oh no, what if this happens?" Your stomach gives a little twist, and a cold wave of fear ripples through you. But then you immediately say to yourself, *I'd better pray about that.* You intentionally bring that matter before Him, and lay it at His feet.

So what's the solution? When your knees start knocking, *kneel* on them! Don't worry. Pray. That's what the Bible teaches.

~

When your knees start knocking, kneel on them!
Don't worry. Pray.

Sometimes when we face adversity or difficulty, we turn to people for help. There is a time and a place for turning to people, but they should not be the *first* place you turn. Others may turn to alcohol, which is never a solution. If anything it only leads to greater problems. We must train ourselves to turn toward God, our heavenly Father who loves us.

The Thanksgiving Factor
Paul is talking about more than just bombarding heaven with our requests. The text says, "In everything by prayer and supplication, *with thanksgiving.*"

Don't miss this. Thanksgiving is a vital component of prayer even before it's answered—*especially* before it's answered. I am taking time to worship my heavenly Father and remind myself of His greatness and power, and in so doing I automatically put my own problems into their proper perspective. As I contemplate the awesomeness and magnificence of God, I see my own life situations in corresponding smallness.

This is why the Lord taught us to pray, "Our Father in heaven, hallowed be Your name. Your kingdom come. Your will be done on earth as it is in heaven.

Give us this day our daily bread" (Matthew 6:9–11).

If *I* had written the Lord's Prayer, it probably would sound more like this: "Our Father in heaven, give us this day our daily bread." You know…just cut to the chase. Here's what I need, God.

But Jesus taught us that before we offer a word of personal petition, we need to utter thoughts like these: "Father, You are in heaven. You are mighty. You are beautiful. You deserve to be revered and worshiped and adored. Father, I just want to do that for a few moments. Before I bring a single request before You, before I talk to You about my own needs and concerns, Your kingdom come, Your will be done on earth just like it is up there in heaven. Lord, if what I'm about to pray is outside of Your will, overrule it. I know that You know what's right and best for me." Praying in that way tends to put everything into perspective.

Have you prayed about your problems? That thing that is troubling you right now, that worry that has been tormenting you? You've been down and depressed and discouraged over it. You've been driven to fits of anxiety and heart-pounding bouts of stress. But have you prayed about it?

Peace on Guard Duty

...let your requests be made known to God; and the peace of God, which surpasses all understanding, will guard your hearts and minds through Christ Jesus. (Philippians 4:6–7)

It's important to note what this passage does and does not say. It does not say you will necessarily receive the specific things you ask for. But it does say that no matter what, God will give you peace in the midst of it.

You might say, "Lord, take this problem away."

He might, and He might not. But know this. No matter what, He will give you peace as you ride out your personal storm.

We need to trust in the plan and providence of God.

I love it when it says, "And the peace of God will keep your heart and mind in Christ Jesus." That

Have you prayed about your problems?

pretty much covers everything, doesn't it? Those are two areas that cause worry. The heart—wrong feelings; and the mind—wrong thinking. God's peace will guard both.

The phrase Paul uses here is a military term. He's saying that God's peace will mount a garrison or literally stand guard around your heart and protect you, if you will present your requests to Him.

Daniel, an Old Testament prophet, was a man who personified these things. He not only prayed every single day, he would open up his windows, get down on his knees and call out to God in plain view of everyone. He had some enemies in the capital of the Persian empire, where he lived, who hated him and wanted him destroyed because he had the ear of King Darius. They looked for scandal in his life but could find none. Finally they decided if they got the king to authorize some crazy law where nobody could pray to anyone but him, they could have Daniel arrested. They brought this proposed law to the king and he absentmindedly signed it, not realizing he was essentially sealing the great prophet's fate.

Daniel heard about it. A decree had been issued that no one could pray to anyone but the king, or he would be thrown alive into the lion's lair.

What would you have done if you were Daniel? You might have said, "I think God would understand if I closed my windows for my prayer meetings from this point on. God can hear me just as well when I pray silently. What's wrong with being a little discreet? Besides, I'm of no use to God if I'm dead, which is what I will be if I'm seen praying."

Sometimes we're embarrassed to pray in public. Maybe you're at a restaurant, the meal comes, and you're embarrassed to bow your head and offer thanks. Maybe you're self-conscious about taking out your Bible during a flight—so you get an "incognito Bible" that looks like a novel or a day planner.

Daniel wasn't embarrassed. And he didn't intend to hide. He made up his mind to pray just as he always

No matter what, God will give you peace in the midst of your struggles.

did. Same place. Same time. Same practice. And sure enough, he was arrested and sent to the den of lions. There was nothing the king could do because he had signed his own decree and could not change it. So God's man spent that night in the close company of some very large, very hungry felines.

Guess who slept soundly?

Guess who was up all night?

The king didn't get a wink of sleep worrying about the Hebrew prophet he esteemed so highly. Daniel, however, slept like a baby.

I figure God's man saw this as a win-win situation. Option 1: He would have a nice night's sleep and use this big old cat as a soft pillow. Option 2: He would be a fast-food dinner for Leo, and wake up in heaven. Either way, he was more than fine. How could he lose?

You know the story of how God preserved the prophet. The lions suddenly lost their appetite when Daniel dropped in as a roommate...only to regain it again (with a vengeance) when his accusers were tossed in afterwards.

This is a classic story of prayer. In Daniel 6, we read that the man of God prayed, gave thanks, and presented his requests to God *after* he found out he could be arrested for it. In other words, he did exactly what Paul tells all of us to do here in Philippians. He prayed and made supplication, and refused to be anxious even when his very life was on the line.

Cast and Care

We need to remember to cast our cares upon the Lord. So many of us drag our cares around all day, gathering more and more of them as the day wears on. Is it any wonder we feel so weary in our soul? In 1 Peter 5:7 we're instructed to "[cast] all your care upon Him, for He cares for you." Two words jump out of this passage: *cast* and *care*. The word *cast* is not the normal word for throwing something. Rather, it is a word that signifies a definite act of the will by which we stop worrying about things and let God assume the responsibility for our welfare.

Then the word *care*, as in "He cares for you," means that He is mindful of your interests. God is concerned about you. If it bothers you, it is of concern to Him. If it is troubling you, He wants to intervene and help you.

~

*What a comfort to realize that God
is thinking about you right now.*

In Psalm 139:17–18 the psalmist says, "How precious are your thoughts about me, O God! They are innumerable! I can't even count them; they outnumber the grains of sand!" (NLT). Then in Psalm 40:17, "As for me, I am poor and needy, but the Lord is thinking about me right now. You are my helper and my savior" (NLT).

What a comfort to realize that *God is thinking about you right now*, and "you can throw the whole weight of your anxieties upon him, for you are his personal concern" (1 Peter 5:7, *Phillips*).

2. RIGHT THINKING

Finally, brethren, whatever things are true, whatever things are noble, whatever things are just, whatever things are pure, whatever things are lovely, whatever things are of good

report, if there is any virtue and if there is anything praiseworthy—meditate on these
things. (Philippians 4:8)

Maintaining personal peace involves both the
heart and the mind. Isaiah 26:3 says, "You will keep
him in perfect peace, whose mind is stayed on You,
because he trusts in You."

What we think about ultimately affects what we
do. For this reason, we must nip in the bud any
thoughts that would be impure, spiritually harmful,
or would feed the beast of worry. Train your mind to
think biblically.

We are told in 2 Corinthians 10:3 that we should
cast down every imagination and every high thing
that exalts itself against God, and bring every thought
into captivity to the obedience of Jesus Christ. Fill
your minds with the things of God.

The next time you find yourself troubled by some
issue in your life, talk to yourself a little! What I mean
by this is we need to train our minds to think biblically, and rein in our emotions accordingly. Faith does
not work automatically. You have to apply it.

Let me illustrate. In Psalm 42, the psalmist is deeply troubled. He is concerned and anxious over something. His emotions seem to be getting the best of him, causing him to cry out, "Why are you cast down, O my soul? And why are you disquieted within me?" (v. 5)

He was talking to himself. Rather than submitting to depression and despair, he began applying faith, reason, and biblical thinking to his situation. He told himself, "Put your hope in God, for I will yet praise him, my Savior and my God" (vv. 5–6, NIV).

Try it! The next time doubt or temptation comes, the next time worry begins clawing at the door of your heart, sit yourself down and have a little chat. *Come on, self. What are you thinking? Snap out of it.* Quote Scripture to yourself. Remind yourself of what is true. Remind yourself of the faithfulness of God in your life through the years.

～

Remind yourself of the faithfulness of God in your life through the years.

Every believer needs to do this. I don't care how many years you've known the Lord. Anyone can experience a lapse of faith—a moment of black despair—when pain intrudes or darkness falls. You can endure a period of life where you feel disoriented and confused. It happens to all of us. I've certainly had my moments, and I'm pretty sure that you've had yours. Even a great patriarch like Abraham experienced seasons of fear, doubt, and internal struggle.

Having faith, however, means you refuse to stress out about your life. You reject the inclination to hold on to dark thoughts about the future. The devil may bomb you with a shock-and-awe campaign, but you are resolute. Having faith means that you say, "I've made up my mind. God help me, I will not let worry rule over me. I've done the right thing. I've done what I believe to be right and legitimate. So I will wait on God and not let stress and second-guessing give me an ulcer or a heart attack."

That's right thinking.

It's interesting to me when I reflect on how God gave His revelation to mankind. How did He do it? Did He give it to us in a picture or a painting? A movie, a music video, or a song? No. He gave us His revelation in book form, in a written word. Why? So that we might think, read, and reason.

Some people will tell you that following Jesus Christ means you're no longer thinking clearly, that you deceive yourself by seeking to serve the living God. Nothing could be further from the truth. The most right-thinking person on earth today is the biblically literate Christian who looks at life in a logical, clearheaded manner through the lens of God's eternal Word. God says, "Come now, and let us *reason* together" (Isaiah 1:18).

More than anyone else—no matter how many doctorates he or she may have—the Christian understands what's going on in the world. We understand that man is inherently sinful, and that technology and "progress" will never solve our problems. Nor will politics or any human-generated solution. We affirm that the only real solution is the intervention of God stepping into time, and that the only way to change human behavior is through an encounter with the living Christ.

In a prayer to His Father, Jesus said: "O Father, Lord of heaven and earth, thank you for hiding the truth from those who think themselves so wise and clever, and for revealing it to the childlike" (Matthew 11:25, NLT).

3. RIGHT LIVING

The things which you learned and received and saw in me, these do and the God of peace will be with you. (Philippians 4:9)

You can't separate outward action and inward attitude. The way you think *is* the way you will live. If you're engaged in right praying and right thinking, it follows that you will be engaged in right living, as a matter of course.

Sin, however, always results in turmoil and unrest. Isaiah 57:20-21 describes the unbeliever. It says,

~

If you're engaged in right praying and right thinking, it follows that you will be engaged in right living.

"The wicked are like the troubled sea, when it cannot rest, whose waters cast up mire and dirt. 'There is no peace,' says my God, 'for the wicked.'"

In contrast, as we live in purity as Christians, we experience God's peace. Isaiah 32:17 says, "The work of righteousness will be peace, and the effect of righteousness, quietness and assurance forever."

Even in the midst of turmoil and craziness the Christian can have the peace that passes all human understanding. I have seen it. I have talked with believers who are terminally ill or facing the most adverse of circumstances, and I have seen that peace in action. I have seen how God can intervene.

There are believing soldiers right now on the battlefield in Afghanistan and Iraq who face death hour by hour, even as you turn the pages of this book. But there is peace in their heart because their life is right with God. Only Christ can give that. The world can't give it. A drug can't give it. Alcohol can't give it. A yoga class can't provide it. Only God can.

And if you ask Him, He will.

GOD'S ANSWER
TO FEAR

AMERICANS USED TO LOOK AT THE VIOLENCE AND terrorist attacks in the Middle East and around the world, and just shake their heads. This was really terrible stuff to read about in the newspapers or see on the evening news, but we told ourselves (if not in so many words), "It could never happen here."

Not anymore!

Our imaginary bubble of "homeland security" burst forever. We realize that our nation is more vulnerable than we ever dreamed.

Our government warns us almost daily about more potential strikes on American soil, or on our nation's interests abroad. Such attacks could spark more fear, sending a message that no place is safe.

Then there is the almost unthinkable concern that a group of these murderous thugs might somehow obtain a nuclear weapon.

Many people are afraid. And with good reason.

FRIGHTENING DAYS

So what are we supposed to do? Find some hole to crawl into, cover our heads, and hope against hope that none of this happens to us?

In the Gospel of John, the Lord gives us some very direct words about facing the times in which we live. He tells us how to function so that we won't be overcome by the threats and anxieties of our times.

"Let not your heart be troubled; you believe in God, believe also in Me. In My Father's house are many mansions; if it were not so, I would have told you. I go to prepare a place for you. And if I go and prepare a place for you, I will come again and receive you to Myself; that where I am, there you may be also. And where I go you know, and the way you know." Thomas said to Him, "Lord, we do not know where You are going, and how can we know the way?" Jesus said to him, "I am the way, the truth, and the life. No one comes to the Father except through Me." (John 14:1–6)

Jesus begins by saying, "Let not your hearts be troubled." Another way to translate that word "troubled" would be agitated, disturbed, or thrown into confusion.

The Lord isn't saying here that we lack reasons to be troubled. What He is really saying is that there is greater reason *not* to be.

We can all acknowledge that life is filled with trouble. The Bible says in Job 5:7, "Man is born to trouble." From the moment you leave the womb you

～

The Lord isn't saying that we lack
reasons to be troubled.

encounter it. (Isn't it classic that life begins with a doctor's slap on our backside? What an introduction!) We have health troubles, family troubles, boyfriend and girlfriend troubles, and financial troubles. Everybody has trouble in life.

We all face almost daily disappointments—some small, and some so large they threaten to crush us. We're unhappy with ourselves because we so rarely live the way we want to live. We want to be strong, but find ourselves weak. We want to be courageous, but feel overcome by fear. We want to be successful, but fail repeatedly. We want to be liked, but so often people seem indifferent to us. We want to live in purity, but cave in too often to impure thoughts and desires.

Jesus tells us, "There are troubles in the world, but don't be agitated and stressed out and thrown into confusion. Though there is reason to be troubled, there is greater reason not to be."

What is that greater reason?

Actually there are three. The Lord gives us a trio of assurances to hold on to during seasons of darkness, pressure, and stress.

1. WE KNOW HIM

"Let not your heart be troubled; you believe in God, believe also in Me." (John 14:1)

"Believe in Me," Jesus is saying. "I've brought you this far, and I have no intention of abandoning you. I know what I am doing. *Believe.*"

In the Greek language, this is a command. The Lord is saying, "I command you to believe in Me."

Why were the disciples stressed out? Because the Lord had just dropped a huge bombshell in their midst. He had just revealed to them that one of their own would betray Him.

Talk about a shocker. These men had been together for three years, sharing everything. It was inconceivable that one of them—one of the Twelve!—would turn his back on the Master. "Who is it? Is it me, Lord?"

~

*The Lord is saying,
"I command you to believe in Me."*

GREG LAURIE

With the advantage of hindsight, we now know that Judas Iscariot was the traitor. Why couldn't these guys figure that out? It seems so obvious to us now. Whenever you're watching a movie about Jesus, you can always pick Judas out of the crowd. He's wearing black, frowns a lot, and skulks around in the shadows.

The fact is, however, that Judas wasn't as obvious as we might imagine. If he frowned or skulked, it didn't concern the others at all. He may have been the *last* one the disciples suspected.

Following this stunning prediction of betrayal, Peter thought he sensed a good opportunity to remind the Lord of his own ironclad commitment. "Though all deny You," he declared, "I will never deny You." Jesus replied, "Peter, not only will you deny Me, you will disown Me three times before the rooster crows tomorrow morning."

More shock! More devastation! It just didn't compute. One of them was a traitor who would betray the Lord. Peter, one of the closest to Jesus, would deny Him. Three times! If these things were true, what about the rest of them? Would anyone make it, or would they all wash out, too?

Understand that these guys were no shrinking violets. They were courageous men. They had faced a great deal of danger and risk following Jesus, standing strong in the face of pressure, criticism, and constant threats. They loved their Teacher and Lord, had left everything to follow Him, and (with the exception of the betrayer) were willing to die for Him if necessary. It wasn't that they were afraid of danger. What alarmed them was the thought of living their lives without Him!

Earlier in John's Gospel, a huge crowd had been following Jesus everywhere. Knowing that most of these people were mere hangers-on—half-hearted followers at best—He deliberately served up some strong teaching, knowing it would thin out the ranks. And that's just what happened. Many of those who had been following the Lord simply turned around and walked away.

At that point, He turned to the Twelve and said, "Will you also go away?"

They said, "Lord, where else will we go? You alone have the words of eternal life." In other words, "Lord, wherever You go, we're going with You. We love You.

We're committed to You. We want to be with You."

That's why they just couldn't believe their ears when Jesus began saying, "I'm about to leave you. One of you will betray Me. One of you will deny Me."

He was saying to them, "Believe in Me. When I tell you I'm about to leave, you have to know it is for a purpose." He was describing His impending crucifixion. He was on His way to fulfill His mission of becoming a sacrifice for the sins of the world, but He would be raised to life three days later.

Today we understand the significance and necessity of all these events. But for that little band of brothers on this particular night in the upper room, this made no sense at all. Zero. Understanding this, knowing full well their grief and devastation, Jesus was telling His men in essence, "When you don't understand what I am doing, you have to fall back on what you do know. I am saying trust *Me*."

~

"When you don't understand what I am doing, fall back on what you know. I am saying trust Me."

There are times in our lives and events in our lives that just don't make sense. Tragedies hit. Sorrows come. Troubles blindside us. We say, "Lord, what's up with this? Why did You let that happen to me? Why did You allow this tragedy to crash into my life? I don't need this! What are You doing here, Lord?"

When I don't understand what God is doing, I have to fall back on what I do understand. And what I do understand is that He loves me, and everything that He allows in my life is run through the filter of His plan and purpose for me. The word *Oops!* is not in God's vocabulary. There are no mistakes in the life of a child of God. I have to trust Him. We must remember that Jesus was not only speaking to these troubled disciples two thousand years ago, but to us as well.

We tend to think in the short-term with our limited view.

We think of the temporal; God, the eternal.

We are thinking of today; God is planning for tomorrow.

We think of comfort; He thinks of character.

We think about the "path of least resistance"; He

is thinking of the paths of righteousness.

All of our stress and agitation and troubled hearts come from ignoring His Word.

2. YOUR DESTINATION IS HEAVEN

"In My Father's house are many mansions; if it were not so, I would have told you." (v. 2)

When we read these words we think of beautiful palatial mansions like we might see in a place like Beverly Hills or some exclusive gated community.

It reminds me of a story about a well-known minister and a New York cabdriver who both died and went to heaven. Simon Peter met them at the Pearly Gates. Approaching the taxi man first, Peter introduced himself and said, "I'm in charge of housing here. I want to direct you to the place we have set up for you." He put his hand on the cab driver's shoulder and pointed into the distance. "You see that mansion over there on that beautiful green hilltop? That's yours, my friend. Go and enjoy it."

The cab driver smiled, tipped his hat, and walked

off with a spring in his step toward his new estate.

At this, the minister stood a little taller. He thought, "If a New York cabbie gets a mansion like that, imagine what I will get!" Peter called the minister forward and said, "See that beat-up shack down there in the valley? That's your place. You go there."

Shocked, the minister said, "Excuse me, Peter. I'm a man of God. I've spent my life in the ministry, serving the Lord and preaching the gospel. I don't understand how a New York cab driver would get a mansion and I would just get a shack in the valley!"

"Here's what it comes down to," Peter replied. "It seems that when you preached, people slept. But when he drove, people prayed."

When we read about mansions, we need to understand that this is most likely *not* a description of buildings. More likely, it describes the new, glorified body God will give us after we die and leave our old body behind. Paul writes:

Our present troubles are quite small and won't last very long. Yet they produce for us an immeasurably great glory that will last forever!

So we don't look at the troubles we can see right now; rather, we look forward to what we have not yet seen. For the troubles we see will soon be over, but the joys to come will last forever. (2 Corinthians 4:17–18, NLT)

Jesus says He is preparing a place for us in His Father's house. Whatever that may mean, we can count on it being more wonderful than we could dream or imagine.

"No eye has seen, no ear has heard, and no mind has imagined what God has prepared for those who love him." (1 Corinthians 2:9, NLT)

It's interesting that the Bible doesn't give us many descriptions of heaven. There are some hints, some quick flashes of its beauty and wonder, but it's all so

~

Jesus says He is preparing a place for us in His Father's house.

difficult for us to grasp. How do you enumerate the infinite to a finite being? It's tough. For God to describe the glories of heaven to someone who has only known the limitations of earth is not an easy thing to do.

It would be like trying to describe the beauty of Hawaii to a three-month-old baby. You prop her up on a pillow. She falls over. You prop her up again, and start to tell her about the warm surf and the blue skies and the white sands. But then you notice she's absorbed in trying to stick her big toe in her mouth.

She just doesn't get it. She can't comprehend Hawaii. She doesn't have the mental capacity yet. And you and I have neither the capacity nor the capability to grasp the majesty and splendor of our eternal home. The apostle Paul had the unique experience of dying, being received into heaven—and then coming back again! (Wouldn't that be a letdown!) He could have come back and written a book, gone on Christian TV, or made the rounds on the inspirational speaking circuit. Instead, all he would say about what he saw on the other side was, "I heard things I can't describe, and I saw things I can't explain. All I can tell you is it was paradise" (2 Corinthians 12:1–4).

Know this much. It's going to be good. Very, very good. Impossibly, unimaginably good. And it's waiting just around the corner for everyone who has placed his or her faith in Jesus Christ.

When you get to heaven, all of your questions will be answered. The Bible says in 1 Corinthians 13:12, "Now we see things imperfectly as in a poor mirror, but then we will see everything with perfect clarity. All that I know now is partial and incomplete, but then I will know everything completely, just as God knows me now" (NLT).

You say, "When I get to heaven, I have a few questions I want to ask God. In fact," you declare, pulling a folded piece of notebook paper out of your pocket, "I have this list."

~

When you get to heaven,
all of your questions will be answered.

With all respect, when you get to heaven, I don't think you'll be checking off items on a list of questions. I think you'll look at last into the face of God and say, "Never mind."

This is the hope that we have—the hope that banishes our worries and fears.

Even though heaven awaits me, I want to live my life here on earth as long as I can live it. I want to take care of myself physically and make wise choices about what I do with my allotment of years. As believers, we want to do everything we can to honor the Lord in all we do, not knowing from day to day how long we'll have that opportunity. What it comes down to is if I die tonight, I will go to heaven. I will be in the immediate presence of my Savior and King.

What's so bad about that? As a Christian, you would step into life eternal. The worst scenario is not dying. You will die no matter what.

The worst-case scenario would be to die without Jesus. If you don't have Jesus, that and that alone is "the sum of all fears." That is why we want to make sure we are prepared to meet God.

THE ULTIMATE ANSWER

As Jesus laid these things out for His disciples, they were completely overwhelmed. They felt like a tsunami had just broken over their heads. Their world seemed to be unraveling before their eyes. One of them would betray Him. One would deny Him. And He was going away, where they could not follow (yet).

These guys were shell-shocked. Troubled. Sick at heart. And He said to them:

> "Don't be troubled. You trust God, now trust in me. There are many rooms in my Father's home, and I am going to prepare a place for you. If this were not so, I would tell you plainly. When everything is ready, I will come and get you, so that you will always be with me where I am. And you know where I am going and how to get there." (John 14:1–4, NLT)

I think the disciples, glassy-eyed, were all nodding their heads.

I also think they were clueless.

I don't think they had any idea what He was talking about.

Picture yourself in the classroom, and your math teacher has just chalked out some complex problem on the blackboard. He turns around and says, "Does everyone understand? Is there anybody that doesn't get it?" You're completely lost at sea, but you don't want to be the only one to raise your hand.

That's how I see this scene.

"Uhhh…right, Lord. That is so deep. Yes."

Thomas, however, ventures to raise his hand and ask the question everyone was thinking but was afraid to ask. "Teacher, we have no idea where You're going, so how could we possibly know the way?" Jesus doesn't criticize him or get mad at him. He says, "Good question. And here's a good answer. I am the way, the truth, and the life. No one comes to the Father, except through Me."

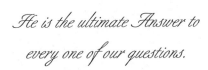

He is the ultimate Answer to every one of our questions.

He is the ultimate Answer to every one of our questions.

And He is the remedy for all of our fears.

LIFE BEYOND THE GRAVE

DEATH, THE GREAT EQUALIZER, IS NO RESPECTER of persons. It doesn't matter if you're young or old, man or woman, rich or poor, famous or unknown, godly or pagan.

Death knocks at every door.

The Bible is very clear about this. In the book of Hebrews we're told that "it is appointed for men to die once, but after this the judgment" (Hebrews 9:27).

Sometimes death comes when it's generally expected, after we've lived a long and full life. At other times death comes abruptly—far too soon in our way of viewing things. Somehow in our minds we feel that both we and our loved ones are entitled to a long life.

But there are no guarantees that any of us will live into old age. We don't know when death will come. The Bible tells us there is a time to be born and a time to die.

USA Today took a poll of its readers, asking the question, "If you could ask God or a supreme being anything, what would you ask Him, knowing that you would get a direct answer?" Many of those polled wanted to know how long they would live.

It truly is a question no one but God can answer. Though the day and hour of our passing has been predetermined, we don't know when it is.

In Job 14:5 the patriarch says of God, "You have decided the length of our lives. You know how many months we will live, and we are not given a minute longer" (NLT).

But none of us know when that day or moment might be.

～

There are no guarantees that any of us will live into old age.

Several years ago, I conducted a funeral service for the crew of Alaska Airlines flight 261. The McDonnell-Douglas MD 83 was on its way from Mexico to Los Angeles when it experienced mechanical problems and crashed into the sea, taking all 88 people on board down with it, including the pilot and crew. There were no survivors.

We were contacted by Alaska Air and asked if they could hold their service in our sanctuary, because they needed a large building in the area where our church was located. We're often asked by different organizations if they can have services in our building. Sometimes we allow it, but always with the condition that one of our pastors is allowed to speak and give a gospel message—because ours is a building set apart for the gospel of Jesus Christ. And the airline agreed to this.

I decided to take this one myself. Alaska Airlines personnel, most in uniform, filled our auditorium some three thousand strong. Sadly, I did not have the assurance that any of the people on that crew were believers. I'm not saying there weren't. There may have been many. It may be that some of them put their faith in Christ while the plane was on its way down. But since I had no evidence that the crew members belonged to Christ, I could not say that I knew these people were in heaven. That made it a very difficult service to perform.

I spoke about the brevity of life and the need to get ready to meet God. It's sad when you can't offer the firm hope of eternal life to grieving people. But only those who have put their faith in Jesus Christ have the solid assurance that they will step into the presence of God when they cross over to the other side.

SLEEPING AND WAKING

That is the hope of the Christian, that death is not the end. That there is life beyond the grave. That the best is yet to come. Because Jesus died and rose again, we have the hope that we will do the same. The apostle declares:

> For our perishable earthly bodies must be transformed into heavenly bodies that will never die.

When this happens—when our perishable earthly bodies have been transformed into heavenly bodies that will never die—then at last the Scriptures will come true:

> "Death is swallowed up in victory.
> O death, where is your victory?
> O death, where is your sting?"

For sin is the sting that results in death, and the law gives sin its power.

Our perishable earthly bodies must be transformed into heavenly bodies that will never die. How we thank God, who gives us victory over sin and death through Jesus Christ our Lord! (1 Corinthians 15:53–57, NLT)

Yes, our bodies will cease to function at some point. But because of the accomplished fact of our Lord's resurrection and victory over this final enemy, those who have put their faith in Christ don't have to be afraid.

In John 14 Jesus said, "I will not leave you orphans; I will come to you. A little while longer and the world will see Me no more, but you will see Me. Because I live, you will live also" (vv. 18–19).

I'm fascinated by how the Bible uses the phrase *falling asleep* to describe death for a Christian. When you're young, you don't like to go to sleep. I still remember when I was in nursery school, having to take naps on little rubber mats they put on the floor after they served us lukewarm milk. How I hated that. I hated to sleep when I was a kid, and I fought it tooth and nail.

As I get older, however, a nap is becoming more and more of a luxury. Now the idea of catching a few winks in the middle of the day is very appealing to me.

The Bible compares death for the Christian to sleep. Just falling asleep and waking up in the presence of the Lord.

LIVE-FOREVER BODIES

And when you do "wake up" in your eternal home, you'll have an incredible surprise. God has a new

THE BEST IS YET TO COME

body prepared for you. The Bible also says of this new body, "For we know that when this earthly tent we live in is taken down—when we die and leave these bodies—we will have a home in heaven, an eternal body made for us by God himself and not by human hands. We grow weary in our present bodies, and we long for the day when we will put on our heavenly bodies like new clothing" (2 Corinthians 5:1–2, NLT).

Not long ago, a six-year-old boy in our church had a question for me.

"My grandmother just died," he told me. "And I was wondering if I would see her in heaven."

Knowing the family, I said to him, "Son, I believe you will see her. But she won't look quite the same as she looked before. Was she ill when she died?"

"Yes. She was very sick."

"Was she wrinkled?"

"Yes, she was."

"Well, she won't look that way in heaven. You'll recognize her, but she will be different because she will be in that new body that God has for her."

The reason this body ages, that hair falls out and we experience sickness, is a result of sin. If Adam and

Eve had not sinned in the Garden of Eden, our bodies would not have aged. We would never experience sickness. But because sin entered into the human race, we all must endure the limitations that it brings to the human body. But in heaven we will possess new bodies that will last forever.

I really like the way Paul compared the experience of receiving our new body to putting on new clothes. Isn't it great when you get a new shirt? Some shirts are so old they're dead. They're so thin and faded you can see right through them. No amount of washing, ironing, or starch will revive them. They're ready for the rag bag. So you pick out a brand-new shirt at your favorite store—all crisp and clean and fresh—and slip it on.

God has a brand-new body for you, and it's better than anything you have ever thought of before. This is the hope we have.

~

God has a brand-new body for you, and it's better than anything you have ever thought of before.

When you go to the theaters, they show previews of coming attractions out there on the cinematic horizon. (Why is it that the real movies never seem quite as good as the trailers?)

God gave us a preview of coming attractions on the day that Jesus died. Matthew 27 describes a very unusual event. It says, "At that moment the curtain of the temple was torn in two from top to bottom. The earth shook and the rocks split. The tombs broke open and the bodies of many holy people who had died were raised to life. They came out of the tombs, and after Jesus' resurrection they went into the holy city and appeared to many people" (vv. 51–53, NIV).

Isn't it wild? Here are people out of the grave, walking around, showing up in unusual places. *Hey, didn't we just bury Uncle Abraham? What's he doing walking around downtown?* It doesn't say everyone rose. But God selected certain godly men and women to be alive again so people could be reminded that death is not the end.

You will live again, and there will be a strong connection between your physical body and your resurrected body. In some ways you will be the same as you are now, and in other ways you will be completely different.

The real you is not what you see in the mirror every morning. Well, yes, in a sense it is: you're looking at the tent in which you currently live. But the essential you that gives you your uniqueness is your personality. Your soul. Your spirit. And when your body dies and goes into the ground, that soul moves on into eternity.

I heard the story of a minister conducting a funeral service. He wanted to say something memorable and profound, but he ended up with a laugh line! Comparing the human body to an external shell, he gestured down to the dearly departed in the casket in front of the church. "Here we have the shell," he said solemnly, "but the nut is gone."

He didn't mean it to come out quite that way! But there was nothing wrong with his theology. The shell stays here; the nut is gone!

Our glorified bodies will be similar to the resurrected body of Jesus Christ. Philippians 3:21 tells us that He "will transform our lowly bodies so that they will be like his glorious body" (NIV). The apostle John assures us that "when He is revealed, we shall be like Him, for we shall see Him as He is" (1 John 3:2).

The resurrected body of Jesus was made of flesh and bones. He wasn't a phantom or a ghost. You couldn't put your hand through His body. Even though He could step into a room without going through the door, He had a warm, solid, touchable human body. Mary grabbed hold of Him, and He said, "Don't cling to Me." Later on, He invited Thomas to put his hand in His side where He had been pierced with a sword, and to touch the wounds of His hands.

In Luke's Gospel we read that He was given a piece of fish to eat. It was a real body, and He wanted His followers (including you and me) to understand that. Jesus said, "Behold My hands and My feet, that it is I Myself. Handle Me and see, for a spirit does not have flesh and bones as you see I have" (Luke 24:39).

~

God will give you a new body—similar to the one you have now…and yet wildly, wonderfully different!

In the same way, God will give you a new body—similar to the one you have now…and yet wildly, wonderfully different! Paul writes: "Our bodies now disappoint us, but when they are raised, they will be full of glory. They are weak now, but when they are raised, they will be full of power. They are natural human bodies now, but when they are raised, they will be spiritual bodies" (1 Corinthians 15:43–44, NLT).

But there's no question these new bodies of ours will be radically improved models! There will be no signs of aging as the millennia roll by. And best of all, I will no longer have a tendency toward sin.

If someone is physically disabled or mentally handicapped here on earth, there will be no such disability in their new body.

Joni Eareckson Tada, a wonderful Christian lady, spoke at our church some years ago. After a diving accident at age seventeen, she became a quadriplegic, without use of her arms or legs, her hands or her feet. In a book called *Heaven: Your Real Home*, she writes about the new bodies God will give to us. She says, "No more bulging middles or balding tops. No varicose veins or crow's-feet. No more cellulite or support hose.

Forget the thunder thighs and highway hips. Just a quick leapfrog over the tombstone and it's the body you always dreamed of. Fit and trim, smooth and sleek."[3]

It's true. The best *is* yet to come.

When we get to heaven, we will want to see one another, and be reunited with loved ones. If you want to look up Greg Laurie, don't go looking for some bald guy. In my glorified body, I will have a full head of hair—maybe even an Afro!

Will we recognize one another in heaven? Of course! Why would we know less there than we know now? Scripture tells us that our present understanding is incomplete. "Now we see things imperfectly as in a poor mirror, but then we will see everything with perfect clarity. All that I know now is partial and incomplete, but then I will know everything completely, just as God knows me now" (1 Corinthians 13:12, NLT).

At the transfiguration of Jesus up on that hilltop, Peter, James, and John recognized Moses and Elijah appearing with Jesus—and I don't think these guys were wearing name tags! ("Hi, I'm Moses.") There was some distinguishing, recognizable factor about these men in their glorified bodies.

We will be with loved ones who have gone ahead of us to the other side. While our family and friends sorrow for you on earth, you will find yourself in new surroundings beyond your imagination. The moment you exhale your last breath on earth, you will inhale your first one in heaven. It's possible that the very angels God sent to protect you throughout your life will then escort you into God's immediate presence—just as they escorted the poor beggar into paradise (Matthew 18:10; Luke 16:22).

Think of the purest joy you have experienced on earth, then multiply that to the tenth power, and you'll begin to catch the tiniest glimpse of heaven's neverending euphoria. David wrote, "In Your presence is fullness of joy; at Your right hand are pleasures forevermore" (Psalm 16:11).

C. S. Lewis made these insightful comments about the glory that awaits the believer.

~

The moment you exhale your last breath on earth,
you will inhale your first one in heaven.

All the things that ever deeply possessed your soul have been but hints of [heaven]—tantalizing glimpses, promises never quite fulfilled, echoes that died away just as they caught your ear.[4]

If I find in myself a desire which no experience in this world can satisfy, the most probable explanation is that I was made for another world.... Probably earthly pleasures were never meant to satisfy it, but only to arouse it, to suggest the real thing.[5]

Not only will we be reunited with loved ones who have gone before us, but we will have the privilege of spending unlimited time with the great women and men of God that He has used throughout the centuries.

Ladies, how about tea with Mary or beauty tips from Queen Esther? Guys, how about building tips from Noah, fishing lessons from Peter—or maybe snorkeling lessons from Jonah!

The radiant light of heaven will last forever. There will be no night, no darkness, no war, no death, no separation, no pain, no tears, no misunderstandings, and nothing to make us afraid ever again. We will have boundless energy and joy in our made-for-eternity bodies. What a day that will be!

"DEATH, WHERE IS YOUR VICTORY?"

Sadly, there are many that don't have this hope, because they have not put their faith in Jesus Christ. As a result, they have a very pessimistic outlook on life in general. For them, it's all in the here and now. There's nothing beyond the grave.

To the modern materialist, death is the cessation of being. Reincarnationists believe that our souls continuously return dressed up in other bodies. (How would you like to be a rhinoceros for a while?) Hindus subscribe to the notion that the body is merely an illusion, and the only thing that ultimately survives is an impersonal cosmic consciousness.

What a bleak outlook! Sometimes I wonder how people with no hope of heaven even manage. In an

~

We know that our present life is just a vapor of smoke that appears for a moment and then vanishes.

interview, actor George Clooney said about life: "I don't believe in happy endings. I do believe in happy travels, because ultimately you die at a very young age or you live long enough to watch your friends die. It is a mean thing, life."

I'm reminded of something Nicolas Cage's character said in the movie *Moonstruck*: "We are here to ruin ourselves, break our hearts, love the wrong people, and die."

That is the viewpoint of the nonbeliever—the man or woman with no hope beyond this life. But that is *not* the viewpoint of the child of God. We know that there is more than this life on earth. We know that our present life—whether it lasts twelve years or 112 years—is just a vapor of smoke that appears for a moment and then vanishes. Scripture describes our time on this earth as a tale that has already been told.

Jesus Christ came to conquer death for us. When

Jesus walked this earth, those who followed Him largely missed His purpose. Even His own disciples failed to grasp what He was saying. They seemed determined to believe that He was about to overthrow Rome and establish His kingdom right then and there. They even had arguments as to which positions they would each play in the new regime. They didn't realize—couldn't imagine—that instead of a crown of gold, He would wear a crown of thorns. Instead of sitting on a regal throne, He would be nailed to a cross of wood. He was not coming to establish an earthly kingdom, He was coming to establish His rule and reign in the hearts of men and women.

They missed it altogether. Jesus had to die to restore lost humanity to Himself. He came to pay a debt He did not owe because we owed a debt we could not pay.

His death and resurrection reverberate to this very day in the twenty-first century. And one of the strongest of those reverberations is that you and I no longer need to fear or dread death. We can look this enemy square in the face and say, "Death, where is your sting, and grave, where is your victory?"

Do you have the hope of life beyond the grave? Has the risen Lord come into your heart yet? One minute after you die you will either be enjoying a personal welcome from Jesus Christ and catching your first glimpse of glory, or you will catch your first glimpse of gloom and despair—as you have never known it. Either way your future will be irrevocably fixed and eternally unchangeable. There is nothing you can do after you exhale your last breath.

In another sense, if you are a believer, you will never die. Jesus said, "I am the resurrection and the life. He who believes in Me, though he may die, he shall live. And whoever lives and believes in Me shall never die" (John 11:25–26).

Let's not misunderstand this. I am not suggesting that we Christians walk around with some kind of a morbid death wish, getting up in the morning saying

~

We know there is purpose and meaning in the lives that we live on this earth.

that we hope we die today. I don't think anyone enjoys or values life more than followers of Christ. We know the God who has made us. We know there is purpose and meaning in the lives that we live on this earth.

We just know we're ready.

And that the best is yet to come.

LIFT UP YOUR HEAD

"I will come again and receive you to Myself;
that where I am, there you may be also."
JOHN 14:3

SOMEDAY, PERHAPS VERY SOON, JESUS CHRIST WILL
step out of heaven and call His own to meet Him in
the clouds.

As we look at the turmoil in our world today, as
we see the continuing conflict in the Middle East, we
realize that Bible prophecy is being fulfilled before our
very eyes.

For instance… The Bible said that the Jewish
people would be scattered to the four corners of the

earth, but would reunite again, and become a nation. Then we're told that this reconstituted nation of Israel would be surrounded by hostile nations who would ultimately rise up against her, but God would intervene for her.

If you had made statements like that back in 1930, people would have thought you had departed from your senses. But on May 14, 1948, that prophecy became a reality. Against all odds, with enemies vastly outnumbering her and seeking to drive her into the sea, Israel once again became a sovereign nation. Since that date, she has been viciously attacked again and again by hostile neighbors. And Israel has not only survived, she has flourished.

Whenever you see conflict in that part of the world, pay attention to the words of our Lord who said, "When these things begin to happen, look up and lift up your heads, because your redemption draws near" (Luke 21:28).

Jesus is coming back again. He could come back today, before the calendar turns another page. Are you ready?

The Bible says He is coming to *receive* us. Notice

~

Jesus could come back today, before the calendar turns another page. Are you ready?

that the Lord says, "When I come, I will receive you unto Myself." You don't have to go with Him if you don't want to go. If you want to stay on the earth and go through the tribulation period, you can. If you want to die and spend eternity without Jesus in hell, you can. God has given you a free will. Or you can place your faith in Him for salvation, and join Him in heaven…forever.

As believers, the hope of our Lord's imminent return is a centerpiece for life itself. All other hopes and desires for the future hinge on *this* hope and desire.

But here's the question.

If we truly believe this, *what effect should it have on our daily lives?* How should looking forward to this greatest of all events change the way we live?

The study of Bible prophecy was never meant to be some academic exercise or intricate brainteaser for puzzle fans who like to play mix and match with Scripture and the headlines. It was meant to change us, to color our every waking moment, to shape our very lives.

We have the strong assurance that our Lord Jesus could return for His church at any moment. And this knowledge ought to motivate us to personal godliness and bold evangelism.

IN THE LIGHT OF HIS COMING

One day as the prophet Daniel pored over the book of Jeremiah in his home in the capital of Persia, a realization hit him like a flash of summer lightning.

He suddenly realized that the seventy-year period of God's judgment on his native Jerusalem was drawing to a close. Would the Lord roll back His wrath and allow a restoration?

How did that fresh understanding of prophecy affect Daniel?

If he had been living today, he might have said, "I think I'll write a bestselling book on that subject—maybe set up a website."

But that's not what Daniel did. Instead, he fell to his knees and began to cry out to God. He writes,

> So I turned to the Lord God and pleaded with him in prayer and fasting. I wore rough sackcloth and sprinkled myself with ashes. I prayed to the LORD my God and confessed: "O Lord, you are a great and awesome God! You always fulfill your promises of unfailing love to those who love you and keep your commands. But we have sinned and done wrong. We have rebelled against you and scorned your commands and regulations. We have refused to listen to your servants the prophets, who spoke your messages to our kings and princes and ancestors and to all the people of the land." (Daniel 9:3–6, NLT)

Daniel's prayer is amazing when you realize that he was a very godly man—one of the few major characters in all the Bible about whom nothing negative is mentioned. Not a single word of criticism. In spite of that, Daniel's study of prophecy moved his heart to repent on behalf of his nation. Instead of being entertained or merely fascinated by his study of future things, he was deeply moved, and prayed with great passion, "O Lord, we repent of our sin."

Is that how you're affected when you think about those coming days of God's judgment on a world that has rejected His Son? Do you find yourself saying, "Yes, Lord, come and judge the world. Zap those sinners, they deserve it"? Or do you pray, "Lord, is there any sin in my life that would displease You? Search my heart, O God"?

It's worth noting that whenever the subject of the Lord's return comes up in Scripture, it's usually accompanied by an exhortation or admonition—some action He wants us to take as a result.

So What?

Over in 2 Peter 3, the apostle tells us that "the day of the Lord will come like a thief. The heavens will disappear with a roar; the elements will be destroyed by fire, and the earth and everything in it will be laid bare" (v. 10, NIV).

You say, well, so what? What does this have to do with me?

Peter goes on to answer that question: "Since everything will be destroyed in this way, what kind of people ought you to be? *You ought to live holy and godly lives* as you look forward to the day of God and speed its coming" (vv. 11–12, NIV, emphasis mine). You see, these prophetic words weren't written for our information, but rather our transformation.

Periodically some kook will come along and he or she will say, "I have cracked the Bible code. I've found messages contained in Scripture that have been hidden from everybody else. Now I'm about to reveal these great truths to you." Or someone else will step in front of a camera on Christian TV and say, "In spite of the fact that Jesus said no man knows the day or the hour of His return, *I* know."

Amazingly, there will always be people who will buy into this stuff. Even people in the church who should know better. They will line up to follow these people. They'll hole up somewhere in the mountains with a bunch of guns, ammunition, and canned food. Or they'll all quit their jobs, put on white robes, grab

some palm branches, and go sit on a hilltop somewhere, waiting for the Lord's return.

But nowhere in the Bible am I told to quit my job
or go hide out in the woods with my ammo and a
copy of *Soldier Weekly*. Instead, the Bible constantly
exhorts me to live a godly life. First Thessalonians 5
says, "Now concerning the times and the seasons,
brothers, you have no need to have anything written
to you. For you yourselves are fully aware that the day
of the Lord will come like a thief in the night. While
people are saying, 'There is peace and security,' then
sudden destruction will come upon them as labor
pains come upon a pregnant woman, and they will
not escape" (vv. 1–3, ESV).

You say, "That's good. So what?" Paul thought of
the "so what." He goes on to say, "But you, brethren, are
not in darkness, so that this Day should overtake you
as a thief. You are all sons of light and sons of the day.
We are not of the night nor of darkness. Therefore let
us not sleep, as others do, but let us watch and be sober.
For those who sleep, sleep at night, and those who get
drunk are drunk at night. But let us who are of the day
be sober, putting on the breastplate of faith and love,

~

*What should we be doing as believers
awaiting our Lord's return?*

and as a helmet the hope of salvation" (vv. 4–8).

In 1 John 3:2 the apostle tells us, "Beloved, now we are children of God; and it has not yet been revealed what we shall be, but we know that when He is revealed, we shall be like Him, for we shall see Him as He is."

So what? How does that affect me? Never fear; John delivers an application no one can miss: "And everyone who has this hope in Him purifies himself, just as He is pure" (v. 3).

Yes, Jesus is coming. And if you believe that, the Bible says that it should directly impact the way you live.

Well, then, what should we be doing as believers awaiting our Lord's return? We who truly believe that the best is yet to come—and that the Best is coming for us...what kind of attitude and mindset should we have while we look forward to that day of days?

Here is what James tells us.

Therefore be patient, brethren, until the coming of the Lord. See how the farmer waits for the precious fruit of the earth, waiting patiently for it until it receives the early and latter rain. You also be patient. Establish your hearts, for the coming of the Lord is at hand.

Do not grumble against one another, brethren, lest you be condemned. Behold, the Judge is standing at the door! My brethren, take the prophets, who spoke in the name of the Lord, as an example of suffering and patience. Indeed we count them blessed who endure. You have heard of the perseverance of Job and seen the end intended by the Lord— that the Lord is very compassionate and merciful. (James 5:7–11)

So what are we to do as we await the Lord's return? James steps up to the plate with some timely advice.

1. BE PATIENT

Therefore be patient, brethren, until the coming of the Lord. (James 5:7)

The word James uses here for "patient" isn't speaking of passive resignation, but rather an on-your-tiptoes
expectancy. He's not saying we should have sort of a
laid-back, laissez-faire attitude: "I suppose the Lord will
show up one of these days. It might be in my lifetime.
I don't know." No, our attitude should be one of anticipation, excitement, and even joy—like a child on
Christmas Eve who can't wait for the morning to come
to open the presents. That's how we should be looking
for the Lord's return. "I can hardly wait. I'm counting
the moments. I welcome that day."

In Romans 13, Paul issues this stirring call to
arms:

The present time is of the highest impor-
tance—it is time to wake up to reality. Every
day brings God's salvation nearer.... The night
is nearly over, the day has almost dawned. (vv.
11–12, Phillips)

Again, what's the "so what" factor here? How does this intersect my daily life? Paul continues,

> Let us therefore fling away the things that men do in the dark, let us arm ourselves for the fight of the day! Let us live cleanly, as in the daylight, not in the delights of getting drunk or playing with sex, nor yet in quarreling or jealousies. Let us be Christ's men from head to foot, and give no chances to the flesh to have its fling. (vv. 12–14, Phillips)

When we twenty-first-century Americans are told to wait for the Lord, it's something of a challenge for us. We live in a culture where everything comes fast. You don't have to wait for anything anymore. If you want something, you don't have to save up your spare change in a piggy bank to purchase it. You don't have to bide your time. You just charge it. Slap it on plastic. And they promise you that you won't even have to make payments for a full year!

We don't want to wait. We want what we want when we want it. We feel we deserve it, whether we

～

When twenty-first-century Americans are told to wait for the Lord, it's something of a challenge for us.

can afford it or not. When it comes to interest rates and monthly payments, we're like Scarlet O'Hara: "I'll think about it tomorrow."

When you're at the supermarket you don't have to wait in long lines anymore. They have an express lane. Of course, I always choose those. Even if I really need more things, I will limit myself to ten items just to get out of there more quickly.

By the way, am I the only person who counts other people's items? *"Hey, what's the deal here? The man has sixteen items! Attention shoppers: There's a man at Register 6 with too many items!"*

We are so impatient. At least I am.

Now, when you pull into some of these fast-food drive-up windows, they have little digital clocks so you can see exactly how long it takes to get your order. You know, today my order took a minute and twenty-eight seconds. But hold on! Yesterday it was a minute and twelve seconds. What's happening here?

We're used to getting everything on demand at breakneck speed—groceries, information, meals...whatever we want.

And then James tells us that we are to "be patient...until the coming of the Lord." We look around at our world and the mess we're in and we say, "Lord, come on! Are You dragging Your feet? Have You forgotten Your appointment? When are You coming back again?"

God has His own schedule—and He's in no way bound by ours. He will come at the time determined in the councils of eternity. He came the first time at the appointed hour, and He will come the second time in the same way.

We are told in Galatians, "But when the fullness of the time had come, God sent forth His Son, born of a woman, born under the law, to redeem those who were under the law, that we might receive the adoption as sons. And because you are sons, God has sent forth the Spirit of His Son into your hearts, crying out, 'Abba, Father!'" (4:4–6).

God watched this little world of ours, and He

knew when the precise moment in time had come. When Jesus arrived on the scene, the people were ready. It had been four hundred years since Israel heard from God, four long centuries since anyone had heard the voice of a prophet or seen an angel or witnessed a miracle. Then John the Baptist burst on the scene telling them that the Messiah had indeed arrived.

Prior to that, of course, at the appointed hour in the little town of Bethlehem, the Messiah was born, fulfilling the prophecy of Micah:

"But you, Bethlehem Ephrathah,
Though you are little among the thousands
  of Judah,
Yet out of you shall come forth to Me
The One to be Ruler in Israel,
Whose goings forth are from of old,
From everlasting." (Micah 5:2)

"From everlasting"…literally, the vanishing point. When the time was just right, Christ was born. The Romans ruled Israel, and Pax Romana was in full force. The armies of Rome had bludgeoned the world into submission. Taxes were high, morale was low, and morals were even lower. And God in His matchless wisdom determined that these were the precise conditions in our world for the entry of His Son.

It will be the same at His second coming. When heaven's clock says so, the Son will return again to this earth. Not a moment too soon. Not a moment too late.

I don't know about you, but it drives me crazy when people are late. If you schedule a time to meet, and your appointment doesn't show up on time, that bugs me. I always try to be on time—or maybe just a little early. When I'm late, it really flusters me. But not everyone! Some people will show up twenty minutes late and won't even say anything about it. And you're just a little bit upset because they didn't keep their commitment to be there when they said they would be there.

Sometimes it may seem to us that the Lord is late. But God reminds us in 2 Peter 3:9, "The Lord is not slow to fulfill his promise as some count slowness, but is patient toward you, not wishing that any should perish, but that all should reach repentance" (ESV).

God is right on time.

His coming may seem to be delayed from our point of view, but we know one thing for sure: We have never been closer to the return of Christ than we are at this very moment. We are nearer to the second coming of our Lord than any generation that has preceded us.

Jesus said, "Behold, I come quickly." He will come when the time is just right.

What else am I to do as I await the Lord's return? The apostle is ready with a second priority.

2. ESTABLISH YOURSELF

Establish your hearts, for the coming of the Lord is at hand. (James 5:8)

Another way to translate this verse is, "Strengthen and make firm your inner life." In other words, *Put iron in your soul.*

The term James uses here is identical to the one Dr. Luke used when he described Jesus' attitudes and actions as He headed toward Jerusalem, knowing full well what awaited Him there.

Of course, Jesus, being God, had full knowledge of all that was about to unfold. He knew Judas would betray Him. He knew He would stand before the high priest Caiaphas. He knew He would be scourged. He knew He would be crucified. And of course, He knew He would rise again from the dead.

But as He set His face toward Jerusalem on that final earthly journey, you can imagine how horrible and appalling all of this was. His humanity recoiled from it. In the Garden of Gethsemane, He poured out His heart in prayer, saying to the Father three times, "Father, if it is Your will, take this cup away from Me; nevertheless not My will, but Yours be done." Yet we are told in Luke 9:51 that as the time approached for Him to be taken to heaven, Jesus resolutely set out for Jerusalem.

That's the word used here for "establish your[self]." Resolutely establish yourself. Stand firm. Take courage. Dig your feet in.

If we were to use the analogy of a plant here, we'd say, "Let your roots go deeply into the soil." The verb conveys the thought of strengthening and supporting something so it will stand firm and immovable.

THE BEST IS YET TO COME

~

God is saying you need to get rooted, because you can count on the fact that your faith will be challenged.

God wants us to be rooted and grounded. Many Christians are not. They have not taken the time to develop habits of personal Bible study or the discipline of prayer in their life or even regular church attendance. They come when it suits them…or when they're in the mood…or when the weather is perfect.

God is saying you need to get rooted, because you can count on the fact that your faith *will* be challenged. You will be persecuted. You will face hardship. Some days are filled with sunshine and others with storms.

And storms can race across the landscape *very* quickly at times—especially if you live in a place like Colorado. Some years ago we held a crusade in Colorado Springs. When we arrived, it was around seventy degrees. There was sunshine on our shoulders, as John Denver used to sing. It was beautiful, and our crusade was to begin the very next evening. As we headed for bed that night, the weather report said a cold front was moving in. I thought, *A cold front. What? Is it going to drop ten degrees? That's no big deal.*

But it was a big deal. The next morning snow covered the ground, and when we held our crusade that night, a strong, icy wind slammed into us. I have never been so cold in my entire life. I put on everything I owned—more layers than you could believe. I even had those little warmer things stuffed in my gloves. And I was still freezing to death.

That's how quickly their weather changes. You look out and the sun is shining. The next thing you know it's a blizzard.

But that's how life can be, too. One moment the weather seems postcard perfect. Then, seemingly in the next instant, the sky grows dark. A cloud comes between you and the sun, and you get some really bad news. Some days it seems to be one thing after another in rapid succession.

These are times when you need to stand firm on the promises of God, when you need to cling to the Lord with your fingers and toes and wait on Him. So listen for His voice. Dig in. Root yourself. And resolutely set yourself to do what God wants you to do.

3. REFUSE TO GRUMBLE

Do not grumble against one another. (James 5:9)

What James describes here is unjust criticism and nitpicking. Biting at each other's heels.

As Christians in a big, wide world, our numbers are relatively small. Yet our task is immense, and time is short. How much of that precious time do we squander, grumbling and complaining and arguing about trivialities and matters of style and opinion, when we should be closing ranks and marching forward? Don't get caught up in that, James tells us.

Remember who the real enemy is.

4. CLING TO YOUR FAITH, REGARDLESS

As you know, we consider blessed those who have persevered. You have heard of Job's perseverance and have seen what the Lord finally brought about. The Lord is full of compassion and mercy. (James 5:11, NIV)

In the life of Job we have a shining example of patience under fire. Job was a man who persevered in times of unbelievable hardship and tragedy.

His story actually begins up in heaven. The angels of the Lord came to present themselves before God, and Satan was among them. God asked him, "Where have you been?" And he answered, "Going to and fro throughout the earth."

You can almost see God pulling on His suspenders as He proudly brags on His servant.

> Then the LORD asked Satan, "Have you noticed my servant Job? He is the finest man in all the earth—a man of complete integrity. He fears God and will have nothing to do with evil."
>
> Satan replied to the LORD, "Yes, Job fears God, but not without good reason! You have always protected him and his home and his property from harm. You have made him prosperous in everything he does. Look how rich he is! But take away everything he has, and he will surely curse you to your face!"

"All right, you may test him," the LORD said to Satan. "Do whatever you want with everything he possesses, but don't harm him physically." So Satan left the LORD's presence. (Job 1:8–12, NLT)

I hate to give the devil his due, but he did bring up a valid point. Many people really do serve or follow the Lord for what they get out of it, and that was Satan's essential argument. "No one serves God for who He is, but only for the goodies he or she can collect." That is tragically true in the lives of many.

But it wasn't true with Job. He was the real deal, a true worshiper. And to prove it to everyone in the spiritual realm (and ultimately our realm this very day), God permitted the crushing calamities that befell this good man in rapid succession. In the space

~

Many people really do serve or follow the Lord for what they get out of it.

of a few moments, Job's world came apart at the seams.

He got up one morning, and it was a day just like any other. The rising sun climbed into the vault of a clear blue sky, and then… A breathless man came running up to Job and gasped, "Someone has just come and taken all of your oxen and donkeys, and they have killed your servants." Before that man even finished his tragic tale, another came and told Job a fire from heaven had fallen and consumed his entire flock of sheep and the attending servants as well. And then yet *another* messenger approached to gasp out the news that the Chaldeans had taken his camels and executed the servants watching them.

If those stunning calamities weren't bad enough, the worst news of all slammed into Job's life like a runaway freight train. Another messenger bore the tidings that all of Job's children had perished in one horrible disaster. The roof of the house where they were dining together collapsed in a violent gust of wind, and no one survived. What could be worse than that?

How would you react to such circumstances? Amazingly, Job did not do what Satan sneeringly predicted he would do. He neither cursed nor renounced his God. But rather, as the Scriptures record, Job tore his robe, shaved his head, fell down to the ground, and worshiped, saying, "Naked I came from my mother's womb, and naked I will depart. The LORD gave and the LORD has taken away; may the name of the LORD be praised" (Job 1:21, NIV).

You say, "That's impossible." No, it isn't. If God in His wisdom would allow you to go through something like that, in His grace He would give you the strength to handle it.

IN THE DARKEST MOMENT

Now God can bring hardship in our lives as discipline as a result of our sin and disobedience. But it certainly isn't always the case, as illustrated in the life of Job. Job was not suffering because of his sin. Job suffered as a righteous man because God allowed it to accomplish a work in his heart that could be done no other way. And since you and I have been in the mind of God before the beginning of time, He allowed His servant to suffer as an example to show that we can endure hardship even if it seems overwhelming.

As you read his book, you will note that Job did ask God why He did certain things, and even said a few things he probably shouldn't have said. But in spite of all of his calamities he never lost his faith. He said in Job 13:15, "Though He slay me, yet will I trust Him."

He ultimately came through it all, saying in Job 19, "I know that my Redeemer lives, and that in the end he will stand upon the earth. And after my skin has been destroyed, yet in my flesh I will see God; I myself will see him with my own eyes—I, and not another. How my heart yearns within me!" (vv. 25–27, NIV).

Job was human like the rest of us. But he kept his priorities straight. He stands as a shining example of faithfulness and patience in trial and hardship. There were lessons that he learned in the valley of despair that can be learned nowhere else. In the end he said,

~

It's always a wonderful moment when a person really opens his or her eyes and meets the living God.

THE BEST IS YET TO COME

"My ears had heard of you but now my eyes have seen you" (42:5, NIV).

It's always a wonderful moment when a person really opens his or her eyes and meets the living God.

Maybe you were raised in a Christian home and heard of the Lord all your life. But there comes a moment when you as a young person say, "Yes, I have heard of Him since I was in the crib. But now I have seen Him. These are *my* truths. I embrace Him as my Savior. Not just as the God of my father and my mother, but as my God."

There are some lessons that can be learned only through experience, through the proverbial school of hard knocks.

Job found that out. And he came through with flying colors.

And in the end, things turned out pretty well for the old boy. God blessed him with more than he had to begin with. More possessions. More livestock. More everything, including a new family. These children, of course, could never take the place of the children who perished. But they must have been a great comfort to Job and his wife for the rest of their days.

Maybe you, like Job, are going through a time of testing and heartache. No, it may not be as dramatic as what he experienced. You haven't lost your home, your livelihood, your family, and your health. But even losing one of those things would be enough! Maybe you just heard bad news and it feels like the ground beneath you is giving way.

What are you to do? Remember these things don't last forever. God will not forget about you in your season of pain. He has an incomparable work that He will complete in your life. The book of Hebrews reminds us that He is "the author and *finisher* of our faith" (12:2). God completes what He begins.

I don't always do that. And I was reminded of that fact just as I was getting ready to leave the house this morning. Putting the milk away, I happened to glance up at the top of the refrigerator and notice a model I had built.

Well…actually, it isn't quite built. It's only about three-quarters done. I meant to finish it three years ago, but kept getting distracted by other things. Then I lost some of the parts. So I've been watching the stores for another model just like it, so I can raid the spare parts and get my little project finished up.

But it hasn't happened yet, and my model has been collecting dust on top of the refrigerator.

Aren't you glad God doesn't deal with us that way? "Oh yeah. Greg. Greg…Laurie, was it? I remember him now. I think I started a work in his life, but I don't remember where the parts are. Maybe I'll get back to him sometime."

God finishes what He begins. He never forgets about you.

> And I am sure that God, who began the good work within you, will continue his work until it is finally finished on that day when Christ Jesus comes back again. (Philippians 1:6, NLT)

～

If Christ were to come back today, would you be ready to meet Him?

So be patient. Establish yourself. Don't grumble. Learn from the example of Job.

Are you prepared for His return? If Christ were to come back today, would you be ready to meet Him? Or let me ask you this: If you were to die today, could you say like Job, "I know that I will see Him. I know my Redeemer lives"?

Maybe you don't know that personally...but you would like to. The same Jesus that was born in that little stable in Bethlehem grew up to be a man, died on a cross to pay the price for all of ours sins, and rose again from the dead. That same Jesus stands at this moment at the door of your heart and life, knocking. He says, "If anyone hears My voice and opens the door, I will come in" (Revelation 3:20, ESV).

Have you ever opened the door of your life and invited Christ in? If not, you can do it today. I hope you will.

Then you too can face life with confidence and joy. And looking out at that hazy horizon in the distance, you can say with a smile, "Life is pretty good right now, and with God's help I'm doing just fine.

"But the best is yet to come!"

NOTES

1. James Montgomery Boice, *The Gospel of John* (Grand Rapids, MI: Zondervan Publishers), 294.

2. C. S. Lewis, *The Problem of Pain* (New York: HarperCollins, 1940), 91.

3. Joni Eareckson Tada, *Heaven: Your Real Home* (Grand Rapids, MI: Zondervan Publishers), 34.

4. C. S. Lewis, *The Problem of Pain* (New York: HarperCollins, 1940), 150–51.

5. C. S. Lewis, *Mere Christianity* (New York: Collier Books, 1960), 120.

Steps to Peace With God

1. ## RECOGNIZE GOD'S PLAN—PEACE AND LIFE

   The message in this book stresses that God loves you and wants you to experience His peace and life.

   The BIBLE says ... For God loved the world so much that He gave His only Son, so that everyone who believes in Him may not die but have eternal life. John 3:16

2. ## REALIZE OUR PROBLEM—SEPARATION

   People choose to disobey God and go their own way. This results in separation from God.

   The BIBLE says ... Everyone has sinned and is far away from God's saving presence. Romans 3:23

3. ## RESPOND TO GOD'S REMEDY—CROSS OF CHRIST

   God sent His Son to bridge the gap. Christ did this by paying the penalty of our sins when He died on the cross and rose from the grave.

   The BIBLE says ... But God has shown us how much He loves us—it was while we were still sinners that Christ died for us! Romans 5:8

4. ## RECEIVE GOD'S SON—LORD AND SAVIOR

   You cross the bridge into God's family when you ask Christ to come into your life.

   The BIBLE says ... Some, however, did receive Him and believed in Him; so He gave them the right to become God's children. John 1:12

THE INVITATION IS TO:

REPENT (turn from your sins) and by faith RECEIVE Jesus Christ into your heart and life and follow Him in obedience as your Lord and Savior.

PRAYER OF COMMITMENT

"Lord Jesus, I know I am a sinner and need Your forgiveness. I believe You died for my sins. Right now, I turn from my sins and open the door of my heart and life. I receive You as my personal Lord and Savior. Thank You for saving me now. Amen."

If you are committing your life to Christ, please let us know!
Billy Graham Evangelistic Association
1 Billy Graham Parkway, Charlotte, NC 28201-0001
1-877-2GRAHAM (1-877-247-2426)
www.billygraham.org